EIGHTEENTH CENTURY SHAKESPEARE

No. 24

General Editor : Professor Arthur Freeman, Boston University

I0591683

An Investigation

O F

Mr. Malone's Claim to the Character

of

SCHOLAR, or CRITIC,

A N

Investigation

O F

Mr. Malone's Claim to the Character of

SCHOLAR, or CRITIC,

Being an Examination of his

INQUIRY INTO THE AUTHENTICITY.

OF THE

Shakspeare Manuscripts, &c.

BY

Samuel Ireland

Routledge
Taylor & Francis Group

LONDON AND NEW YORK

First published by

FRANK CASS AND COMPANY LIMITED

Published 2016 by Routledge
2 Park Square, Milton Park, Abingdon, Oxfordshire OX14 4RN
711 Third Avenue, New York, NY 10017

First issued in paperback 2016

Routledge is an imprint of the Taylor and Francis Group, an informa business

| First edition | 1796 |
| First edition with a new preface | 1970 |

ISBN 13: 978-1-138-97332-9 (pbk)
ISBN 13: 978-0-7146-2512-6 (hbk)

PREFACE

Samuel Ireland's *Investigation* purports to refute
An Inquiry into the Authenticity of Certain Miscellaneous Papers . . . attributed to Shakespeare, &c.
by Edmond Malone, 1796, which had effectively
destroyed all confidence in the 'Shakespearean'
manuscripts forged by Ireland's son William
Henry. In spite of the abject recantation in print
by the latter (which Samuel obstinately disowns
on pp. iv–vi here) following a catastrophic
reception for his *Vortigern* in the stage (2 April,
1796), the father retained lifelong faith in the
forgeries which he had published, and in the two
mock-Shakespearean 'discoveries' of *Vortigern*
and *Henry II* which he would likewise cause to be
published in 1799. Malone's voluminous critique
had appeared on the very eve of the performance
of *Vortigern*, and Samuel Ireland is reported to have
personally circulated handbills at the theatre
attacking Malone (it is typical of the inadequate
modern treatment of these episodes that a recent
historian has it Malone who did the canvassing
at Drury Lane, not *vice versa*); but this *Investigation* constitutes Ireland's full, if futile,
answer to the learned charges. Despite his claim
that he has 'scrupulously abstained from the
declaration of any opinion respecting the authenticity of the manuscripts themselves', and has
concentrated instead upon exposing 'the incom-

petency of Mr. Malone as a man of learning,'
Ireland's arguments all tend, of course, to the
exoneration of his own collection, and it is essential
to read Malone's own words to appreciate fully
the selectivity of Ireland's counterattack, and his
warping or overstatement of Malone's assertions.
Yet this reply is of value in its exemplification of
the very attitudes and methodologies of antiquarian scholarship which Malone himself was
helping to obviate.

An Investigation is undated, but may safely be
assigned to late 1796 or 1797. The paper is
watermarked 1796. The collation is slightly odd,
owing to the cancellation of leaf A1, very likely
as much to tone down the gratuitous arrogance
of line 14 as to replace the heading ('A Reply
to An Enquiry [sic], &c.') with 'An Investigation,
&c.' Thus [ ]2 of the first gathering is signed A
(the cancellans), and [ ]3 a2; normally, then, the
volume contains (as do both British Museum
copies), three preliminary leaves and a cancelled
A1, perhaps indicating that [ ]⁴ was set late or
last, after the imposition of the main text, a not
infrequent practice of earlier printers. Our copy-
text, however, a Folger Library duplicate in the
possession of the publishers, contains both
cancellans and cancellandum, and collates
[ ]⁴A–T⁴[ ]² [T2 mis-signed T3], the terminal
half-sheet being printed on paper different from
the rest. Cancellans A1 has been replaced here
by the corrected leaf, but the uncorrected original
is reprinted as an appendix.

May 1969   A.F.

A N

INVESTIGATION

O F

Mr. Malone's Claim to the Character

O F

SCHOLAR, or CRITIC,

Being an Examination of his

INQUIRY INTO THE AUTHENTICITY.

OF THE

Shakfpeare Manufcripts, &c.

B Y

SAMUEL IRELAND.

———————————

LONDON:

PUBLISHED BY R. FAULDER, NEW BOND STREET;
T. EGERTON, WHITEHALL; T. PAYNE, MEWS GATE;
AND WHITES, FLEET STREET.

PREFACE.

I SHOULD not have been defirous of reviving a controverfy, which has for fome time ceafed to occupy the public attention; or of entering into a difcuffion which the illiberal part of the world has caught at, for the purpofe of indulging its natural propenfity to malevolence; and which a vain, weak, interefted, and illiberal individual has ufed for the purpofe of invading the peace of a private family, by introducing topics to which that difcuffion has no reference whatfoever. But I felt I had a right to expofe the incompetency of Mr. Malone as a man of learning, upon

a 2 the

the only fubject which he affects to know;
and I more ftrongly felt it a duty to expofe
his unworthy, and difingenuous conduct, as
a Man. This object has led me into inquiries which could not be purfued without confiderable diligence and labor. Yet though I
have entered into minute refearches, for the
purpofe of controverting the pofitions of this
Gentleman, I have fcrupuloufly abftained
from the declaration of any opinion refpecting
the authenticity of the manufcripts themfelves. I prefume not to difturb the judg-
ments of the public, if they have formed
any, relative to the origin of the papers.
The truth may probably be afcertained at
fome future period, when literary animofities
fhall have fubfided, and the queftion fhall
have been taken up by lefs interefted and
more temperate enquirers.

It may be expected of me upon this occafion, to fay fomething upon a narrative and
confeffion recently laid before the public.

And

And near to me as by the ties of nature the author of that narrative is, it muft be with fincere regret that I feel myfelf compelled to announce that he withdrew himfelf from my houfe and family in the beginning of June, 1796, that during this period, no intercourfe beyond a fhort communication at two different times, but neither of them under my roof, in the prefence of third parties has fubfifted between us. Whatever meafures therefore, he has taken, relative to the elucidation of the fubject, and of whatever interpretation his conduct may be fucceptible, cannot in the leaft affect me; fince he has been neither open to the remonftrances, nor influenced by the admonitions, which the moral and natural authority of a parent might have fuggefted on my part. And as to his confeffion, whether it receives credit, or whether it be altogether difbelieved, it does not affect the argument which I have offered in this tract. I have merely confidered the reafon-

ings

ings of Mr. Malone on the refpective topics, which have arifen out of the controverfy. I have attempted to prove that he is a bad reafoner, and a futile critic, and that the general inference, which he has drawn as to the authenticity of the manufcripts (whether true in fact or otherwife) is by no means eftablifhed by that mode of proof which he has adduced, and the arguments he has ufed.

A N

AN

INVESTIGATION, &c.

THE greateſt difficulty which I have to en-
counter, in my examination of Mr. Malone's
work, is that which ariſes ftom the ſuperfluous
matter, with which it abounds. The advantage
which that author derives, from this redundant and
deſultory method of purſuing his ſubjeƈt, is very
obvious. If he does not overpower his adver-
ſaries, he at leaſt overwhelms his readers. They,
who take up the book, not indeed from its bulk,
but from the amplitude of its materials, are diſ-
poſed to feel a prepoſſeſſion in its favour; for
where much labor has been obviouſly beſtowed,
ſome learning is neceſſarily inferred. Thus the
greater part of its readers are ſtupified into aſſent,
and are perplexed into acquieſcence; becauſe they
are willing to give the author credit for having
proved that, which their own indolence will not
ſuffer them to examine.

A

Before

Before however, the opinions of any critic are examined, it is proper to fee, whether he has any right to maintain an opinion at all. On what grounds does the critical competence of Mr. Malone reſt? In the beginning of his work he declares that he refuſed to infpeƈt the papers; that he rejeƈted every invitation for that purpofe. He has himſelf pleaded his own difqualification.

All human opinion is the refult of antecedent enquiry; and any opinion on any ſpecific queſtion, may be pronounced ſolid, or ill founded, according to the means and opportunities, which he who maintains it has had of enquiring into the evidence relative to it. Different queſtions require different evidence, and are tried by different ſenſes; but on queſtions concerning certain viſible and material inſtruments, infpeƈtion is the only ſtandard to which reference is to be made. The eye alone examines into the evidence, becauſe it is only by the eye, that minute analogies can be remarked, and compariſons of colors, ſhades, and reſemblances fairly and accurately made. Mr. Malone ſays that he difdained to try this queſtion by perfonal infpeƈtion. He rejeƈted the only fair, and ſatisfaƈtory method of arriving at a judgment upon the papers. Mr. Malone has therefore proved himſelf very incompetent to pronounce concerning their merits.

It

It is worth while to remark the words of Mr. Malone on this curious topic. " I very early re-
" folved" he fays " not to infpect them at the
" houfe of the poffeffor, and I was glad to find
" that my friends Dr. Farmer, and Mr. Stevens
" had made the fame determination; from an ap-
" prehenfion that the names of perfons, who
" might be fuppofed more than ordinarily con-
" verfant with the fubject of thefe MSS might
" give a countenance to them, to which from the
" fecrecy that was obferved relative to their dif-
" covery, they were not intitled." " I was un-
" willing that my name fhould directly or indi-
" rectly give the fmalleft fanction to thefe papers."

Upon this arrogant remark of Mr. Malone, I have only to obferve, that had I imagined that Mr. Malone's infpection of them would have given any fanction to the papers, I fhould certainly have deemed it advantageous to my own intereft to have invited him. But Mr. Malone, and I are of a different fentiment with regard to the fanction, which his infpection would afford them. Of Dr. Farmer I had a different opinion, and I was defirous he fhould examine them. Dr. Parr wrote him a long letter in my houfe, preffing him to come to London for this purpofe, and urging him to view the papers as a duty he owed to himfelf and the world. I mention this to fhew,

that

that I did not fhrink from the fcrutiny of thofe who, converfant with thefe fubjects could have infpected them with an eye of intelligence.

But, in point of fact, did Mr. Malone re-fufe as he infinuates, to infpect thefe pretended originals? I am at iffue with him on the fact. Mr. Malone was not invited to infpect the MSS, but notwithftanding his affertion to the contrary, he betrayed a more than ordinary folicitude to fee them, both by letter, and by the moft preffing application to various perfons : thefe folicitations were fruitlefs, he was informed that he could not be permitted to fee the papers, nor would they be fuffered to pafs out of my poffeffion into any hands; unlefs I fhould receive the commands of any part of the royal family, who might exprefs a wifh to fee them.

Notwithftanding this information through ano-ther channel (that, to which he alluded in his note, p. 22), he earneftly intreated a friend to procure Lord Southampton's letter, and fome of the other papers to be brought up to his houfe at a ftated time, in order that he might compare them with other documents in his poffeffion : re-quefting that his name might not even be men-tioned, as having made the requeft.

The inftrument through which this intrigue was to be carried on, was my fon; and I will leave the

conduct

conduct of Mr. Malone, in reforting to fuch an ar-
tifice, with no other comment, than that which
muft naturally arife from the mere ftatement of
the circumftance.

From what I have faid upon this topic, it muft
neceffarily be inferred, that Mr. Malone is not
always accurate in the ftatement of his facts.
There is a fimilar inaccuracy in the very beginning of his work. He there ftates that his friend
Lord Charlemont fubfcribed to the work, at the
requeft of a gentleman who furnifhed him with a
fplendid profpectus of it ; and " that if Lord
" Charlemont had known as much of it as he now
" does, he would not have given his name or his
" money to the publication." In reply to this,
I can poffitively affert, that I never made any
perfonal application for fubfcriptions to his Lordfhip, or any other perfon whatever. The fact is,
that Mr. Rowley, (I believe a member of the Irifh
Parliament), called upon me to infpect the papers,
and requefted me to put down his name as a fubfcri-
ber, and the name of Lord Charlemont; at the
fame time this gentleman remarked that his noble
friend was not a believer in the authenticity of the
papers. I have ftated this trivial circumftance to
fhew that the infinuation of Mr. Malone is not
founded on truth; that his Lordfhip was not impo-
fed upon by any reprefentations, either in the profpectus

fpectus or by any other channel; but that he voluntarily fubfcribed, with a declaration that he was not a believer.

Before I proceed to follow Mr. Malone, according to the diftribution he has made of the fubject, I would wifh the reader to obferve the temper, with which it fhould feem he fat down to the enquiry. In the firft pages of his work, there is as profufe a portion of egotifm and vanity to be obferved, as I ever remarked in any literary controverfy. His own capacity, as an illuftrator of Shakfpeare, his own poffeffion of the documents relative to the bard, feem to be the only ftandard, by which he tries the merits of the controverted papers. He feems to have entered into the difpute, as if every thing that belonged to Shakfpeare was his own exclufive property; and that any thing relative either to the life, or the writings of that immortal poet which proceeded from any other fource, was an infringement of his own appropriate and inconteftable privileges. He fays with a modefty peculiar to himfelf, " I truft " I fhall not be charged with any idle vanity, a " weaknefs, if I at all know myfelf, moft foreign " from my nature and difpofition." After this profeffion of diffidence, it is amufing to follow the critic into the minute detail with which he favours his readers, of all that he has done as a commentator

tator of Shakfpeare ; a detail, in comparifon of which Mr. Vicary's panegyric on his incomparable tétes, or Mr. Packwood's eulogium on his own razors, is the very refinement of modefty and delicacy. He is perpetually ringing in the ears of the reader, the antient documents of which he is in poffeffion. But till thefe documents are laid before the world, and an opportunity of examining their force, and authenticity be prefented to the public, it is furely a little too unreafonable to expect that they fhould be allowed to be the only teft, by which all enquiries of this nature are to be examined. When the twenty ponderous volumes, with which the public is threatened make their appearance, we fhall then be able to judge concerning the ineftimable treafures of the critic. In the mean while, the ftate of mind in which the author of the enquiry has entered into the inveftigation, muft appear not to be very difinterefted, when he virtually confeffes that he has entered into it, on no other principle, and with no other feeling but that of an offended pride, and an unreafonable vanity, which has taught him to imagine that the very name of Shakfpeare is not to be pronounced without his licence or indulgence.

I fhall now follow Mr. Malone, according to the method in which he propofed to examine the fubject. The firft article which he has felected

for

for animadverfion, is what he is pleafed to call the pretended letter from Queen Elizabeth to Shakfpeare.

" Wee didde receive youre prettye verfes
" goode Mafterre William through the hands of
" oure Lorde Chambelayne ande wee doe com-
" plemente thee onne theyr greate excellence.
" Wee fhalle departe fromme Londonne toe Hamp-
" towne forre the holidayes where wee fhalle ex-
" pecte thee withe thye befte actorrs thatte thou
" mayfte playe before ourefelfe toe amufe uffe bee
" notte flowe butte comme toe uffe bye Tuefdaye
" nexte, affe the Lord Leicefterre wille bee withe
" usse."

Elizabeth R.

" For Mafter William Shakfpeare, atte the
" Globe bye Thames."

" Thys letterre I dydde receyve fromme mye
" mofte gracyoufe Ladye Elyzabethe, ande I doe
" requefte itte maye bee kepte withe alle care
" poffyble."

W. Shakfpeare.

This letter Mr. Malone profeffes to try according to three different teftimonies; the orthography

thography, the phrafeology, the date, and the dif-
fimilitude of the hand writing. But previous to
his entering on the fubject, according to this plan
of difquifition, he indulges himfelf with a few
preliminary remarks; which though they are rather
curious in themfelves, than illuftrative of the fubject, it may be fomewhat amufing to examine.
With much folemnity we are referred to what the
critic ftyles the archetype of this pretended letter,
and the model on which it was conftructed. It
cannot be denied, that Mr. Malone would have
made a very important difcovery, had he ftumbled
upon any antient form of a letter, of which this letter from Elizabeth, was the indifputable imitation
or counterpart. But the refemblance muft be
complete; if it is not complete, no inference can
be drawn from it. No loofe analogies, no general fimilitude, nothing fhort of a perfect identity
will juftify any inference of this nature. Yet what
is the ground, on which Mr. Malone fuppofes
that this letter had an archetype or model, from
which it was derived? Why, it feems that in the
year 1710, Bernard Lintot publifhed an edition
of Shakfpeare's plays, and that in the preface to
that publication, it was for the firft time mentioned that " King James I. honored Shakfpeare
" with an amicable letter written with his own
" hand, and that this letter remained long in the
B " hands

" hands of Mr. D'Avenant, as a credible perfon
" then living could well teftify." Sir William
D'Avenant having died inteftate and infolvent, and
his goods having been feized by his creditors, this
letter was unfortunately loft, and I fear will never
be recovered. Here we have the germ and firft
principle of the letter from Elizabeth to Shakfpeare, now before us.

So then, becaufe King James wrote a letter
to Shakfpeare, it is to be inferred that Elizabeth
could not write one alfo. If Mr. Malone believes
that King James could condefcend to write to
Shakfpeare, furely a *fortiori* it may be prefumed,
that Elizabeth, whom the hiftorians defcribe as
having more condefcenfion of manners than her
fucceffor, might write to her favorite poet, in the
familiar terms of the preceding letter. Then our
critic is pleafed to obferve, that the fabricator of
thefe papers could have had no archetype (except
her fign manual), for the hand writing of Queen
Elizabeth; and therefore that the imitation is
clumfily executed. With regard to this objection,
I can pofitively affert that there are in many private, and public collections, a variety of papers,
moft unqueftionably the hand writing of Elizabeth;
that I have in my own poffeffion many fpecimens
of this kind; and that he muft have been a very
ftupid fabricator, who could not find autographs
of

of the Queen's fign manual, and execute the tranfcript with fufficient exactnefs for his purpofe. But I would wifh the reader to compare the autograph, which appeared in my publication, and to which Mr. Malone applies the terms " irregularity, " and licentioufnefs," with that which he himfelf has exhibited. Surely the difference is fo minute that it would be the height of abfurdity, to build an objection upon it. For when this fac-fimile is compared with that of Mr. Malone's, there is no other difference to be found, but what might be difcovered in the hand writing of any perfon whatever, when the difference of time and circumftances is taken into confideration. At one time, the Queen may be fairly fuppofed to have written with the greateft care and exactnefs; at another, *currente calamo*; and yet the fpecimens may bear a general refemblance to each other. Mr. Malone fays, that he " has perufed from the time of Henry " IV. I will not fay feveral hundreds, but feveral " thoufand deeds, and other MSS." But I much doubt, whether if he had feen them, he could have underftood them; as I have been credibly informed that he cannot eafily or readily, decypher the common hand writing even of the time of Henry VIII.

We now come to the orthography. Our critic obferves that the fpelling of this letter, as well as of the other papers, is not only, not the orthogra-

phy

phy of Elizabeth, or of her time, but is for the
moſt part the orthography of no age whatſoever.
He then animadverts on the redundancy of vowels
and conſonants in the Shakſpeare papers ; and has
exhibited ſpecimens of orthography from the time
of Chaucer to near the end of the ſixteenth century. In p. 74, we are favored with a liſt of words
in the MSS that it is ſaid are not to be found ſo
ſpelt any where elſe. Now it unfortunately happens that in the vocabulary that follows, examples of moſt of them are adduced. And though
Elizabeth did not ſpell the word *and* cr *for*
with the e final *ande, forre,* yet in a letter of hers
to Mary, for which ſee Curioſities of Literature, vol. 2, p. 306, there are the following inſtances of her uſing the e final, and of other ſpelling
which ſeems to correſpond with the fac ſimile of
her letter, riche, greate, beinge, dothe, aſkinge,
thinge, deſiringe, ſelfe, wiche, mynde, towarde,
outwarde, hathe, bothe, ende, longe, &c. &c. I
ſhall take the liberty in my turn, not to quote from
the time of Chaucer, but to exhibit ſpecimens of
ſpelling during the period, on which we are immediately occupied, in which it will be obſerved that
this redundancy of ſpelling, was very common in
thoſe times. In proof of this from many hundred
inſtances the following are ſelected as ſufficient
teſtimonies.

The

The words marked thus * are introduced in Malone's table of inftances to prove the fpurioufnefs of the Queen's letter, under an infinuation that they are no where elfe to be found. Obferve, the inftances here quoted are from printed books; and no doubt but in MSS of that day, many more inftances might be adduced.

Adieu. From Nicol's Elizabeth's Progrefs. p. 2, and in Churchyard's Pleafant Comedy. My deare, *adieu*.

* Atte. See Mafon's Effay on Defign in Gardening, p. 172, and 182. See alfo Sir Richard Guyldford's Pylgrymage towards Jherufalem, folio 43, printed 1511.

Att. Lodge, vol. 2, p. 148.

Awenfuers, (for anfwers). Lodge's Illuftrations, vol. 2, p. 182.

* Ande. See Percy's Ballads, 4 Ed. 1794, p. 136, and 137, and Notes in p. 94, and 95.

Ande. See Gentleman's Magazine for May 1796.

Ande. See Lodge's Illuftrations, vol. 1. p. 22.

Archebifhop. ditto, vol. 1, p. 301.

Broffe of doggs, (for brace of dogs). ditto, vol. 2. E 204.

Bee, (for be). Elizabeth's Progrefs, vol. 2, p. 60.

Bee. ditto, Pennant's London, p. 151.

* Before. Alviarie, 1580.

Bufhopp.

Bufhopp. Lodge, vol. 2, p. 48

Bawbles. See Life and Reign of Richard II. printed in 1681, p. 228, line 17.

Baubles. See Cymbeline, and in a Note by Stevens to the 91ft Sonnet in *Malone's own Edition*.

Clappe. Elizabeth's Tranflation of Seneca. See Nugæ Antiquæ.

Contempne. ditto,

Contynewaynce. ditto.

Clowdes. ditto.

Comhawendemente. From an ancient MS relative to the Howard family, in the 15th, century.

Cuntree, (for country). See Lodge, vol. 2, p. 43. From Elizabeth's own hand writing.

Clenged, (for cleaned). Lodge, vol. 2, p. 101.

Canne. ditto, p. 249.

Cuppe. ditto, p. 252.

Cownfaille. ditto, p· 188.

Coockoes. See Elizabeth's Progrefs, vol. 2.

* Doe. Elizabeth's Progrefs, vol. 2, p. 62, and in State Papers, p. 316.

* Doe. Water Poet, Pennant's London, and Stafford's Niobe.

Doonn, (for done). ditto, p. 316.

Doone, (for ditto). ditto, p. 155.

Daindgeroofly. ditto, vol. 3, p. 22.

Dyfkreete. ditto, vol. 2, p. 67.

Dowbtte. ditto, vol. 3, p. 26.

Dyffave,

Dyſſave, (for deceive). ditto, vol. 2, p. 256.

Depelyer, (for deeper). ditto, vol. 2. p. 185.

Dramme. George Gaſcoine's Works.

Doompes, (for dumps). ditto.

Determynacions. Burleigh's State Papers, p. 321.

Exequuted. See Lodge, vol. 2, p. 39.

Exampell. ditto, p. 183.

Erre. ditto, p. 221.

Empploye. vol. 2, Lodge, p. 162.

Ferre, (for far). ditto, p. 5.

* Forre. See the Fflores of Ovide, printed in 1513, and Waldron's Literary Muſeum, printed in 1792,

Forbydde. Lodge, vol. 2, p. 250.

Fowerttien, (for 14). ditto, p. 144.

Faythebrekynge. vol. 3, p. 59.

Farre. See Conveyance from Walker to Shakſpeare.

Farre. See Nicol's Progreſs, in Verſes on the Coronation of Ann Boleyn.

Fryndeſhippe. Warton's Hiſtory of Engliſh Poetry, vol. 3, p. 423.

* Goode. Lodge, vol. 1, p. 306.

Gonne. ditto, p. 47.

Gracioofs, (for gracious). ditto, p. 75.

Grace. Frequently applied to Queen Elizabeth, in Nicol's Progreſs.

Gemme.

Gemme. Nicol's Churchyard's Pleafant Con-
ceits, p. 5.

Hellpe. Lodge, 1570, N. p. 25.

Hufe, (for ufe). See a MS letter from the
Mayor of Doncafter, in the Shrewfbury Papers, in
the Heralds College.

Howfe. Lodge, p. 38.

Horsfkeippar. ditto, p. 53.

Hadd anny. ditto, 120.

Horffe. Letter from the Lords of the Council to E. of Shrewfberry, 1596. Lodge, vol. 3,
p. 34.

Hee. Brown's Paftorals, p. 2.

I ame, (for I am). Lodge, vol. 2, p. 32.

I mooft, (for I muft). ditto, p. 123.

Juftycefhyppe. ditto, vol. 3, p. 27.

Jerkins of Velvet. Elizabeth's Progrefs, p.
53, among Remarkable Events in 1559.

Knaifferie, (for knavery). Lodge, ditto, p. 79.

Lordfhyppe. ditto, p. 33.

Lieffetenant. Nicol's Churchyard, p. 35,

Myfcontentydde. Lodge, folio 47. 1559.

Mee. ditto, p. 19.

Manne. ditto, p. 249.

Mee. Taylor, Water Poet, 245

Mefter for Mafter. Burghley's State Papers,
445.

Monneth.

Monneth, (for month). Lodge, vol. 1, p. 316, 343.

Nues, (for news). Lodge, vol. 2, p. 64.

Nuers evyn, (for new years evening). ditto, 115.

Nyte, (for night). ditto, 200.

Nienttien, (for nineteen). ditto, 144.

Noe. ditto, 161.

Ourſelfe. Henry VIII. Preface to his Seven Sacraments, printed by Bartelet, 1543, p. 2 and 98.

   * Oure. La Vieux, Nat. Brev. p. 219, 1580.

One, (for on). Malone's Prologomena, p. 484, vol. 2.

Onne, (for one). State Papers, p. 166.

   * Off. Lodge, vol. 1. 128.

Patronne. ditto, p. 48.

Purſſe. ditto, 204.

Putte. ditto, ditto, 250.

Purpoſſe. ditto, 54.

Pryceſſe, (for prices). ditto, 151.

Rangk, (for rank). Lodge, vol. 2, p. 47.

Redyneſse. Elizabeth's Tranſlation of Seneca. See Nugæ Antiquæ.

Sonne. Lodge, vol. 2, p. 3.

Synnes. ditto, 16.

Shoolde. ditto, 35.

Sowne. ditto, 48.

Seemes.

Seemes. ditto, 435.

Soomerz, (for Summers). See Gascoigne's Works. Princely Pleasures of Kenilworth Castle.

Shee. Taylor, Water Poet, p. 258.

Starre. Elizabeth's MSS. Pennant.

Thenne. Lodge, vol. 1. p. 78.

Toowardes. ditto, p. 29.

Tenne. ditto, p. 144.

Uppe. ditto, p. 158.

Usse, (for use). See Darell's Account of Grievous Vexations of seven Persons of Lanca-shire.

Vertuouoose. Lodge, vol. 3, p. 28.

Veu, (for view). Spenser.

Viewe. Queen Elizabeth's Progress, p. 2.

Wytnesses. Lodge, p. 344.

Woorsse, (for worse). Lodge, vol. 2, p. 15.

Woolde. ditto, p. 19.

Warres. ditto, p. 100.

* Wee. Elizabeth's Progress, vol. 2, p. 62.

* Wee. Taylor, Water Poet, p. 195.

* Wee. State Papers, p. 360.

* Wee. Stafford's Niobe, printed in 1611.

* Where. See Barrett's Alvearie, 1580.

* Withe. Bacon's State Papers, p. 315.

Yett. Lodge, vol. 2, p. 35.

Yee. Brown's Pastoral, B. 2, p. 8.

* Yourre. 1559, see Lodge, p. 47.

If Mr. Malone wants MS proofs of a bad and indefinite mode of fpelling, fpecimens enough may be found in his 2d vol. of Prologomena, p. 447, and in his extracts from a vol. of Henflowe's Notes, and Theatrical Accounts from 1597, to 1603.

Mulomurco, for Mulamulluco.
Spanes, for Spanifh.
Malltufe, for Malta.
Poope, for Pope.
Tamberzanne, for Tamberlane.
Gelyon, for Julian.
Janeway, for January.
Burdocks, for Bourdeaux.
Konkerer, for conqueror.
Heafter, and Afheweros, for Efther, and Aha-
fueras.
Camdew, for Candia.
Foftoffe, for Fauftus.
Grefyan, for Grecian.
Umers, for humors.
Anteckes cootes, for anticks coats.
Pygge, for Pfyche.
Anfhente, for ancient.
Serpelowes, for furplice.
Dowlfen, for dauphin.
Fayeton, for Phaeton,

C 2   Mought,

Mought, for mouth.

Apelles, for apples.

Bengemyn, for Benjamin.

Hoate, for hot.

One, for on.

Adycians, for additions.

Hinchlow, a proper name, for Henflowe.

Fower, for four.   p. 493, ditto

Twooe, for two.

From the catalogue I have given, I prefume that Mr. Malone's objection to the letter of Elizabeth on the grounds of its orthography, being irreconcileable to the orthography of the age, is completely invalidated. But our critic lays much emphafis on the objectionable fpelling of the word Mafterre, and remarks that the fpelling of the word at that period was *Maifter*. Yet notwithftanding the decifive tone of this affertion, he himfelf produces an inftance in p. 377, of his appendix, of its being fpelt Mafter.

In the Pafton Letters, 2d vol. p. 292, he likewife confeffes that it is fpelt Maftyr, and in the Burleigh State Papers it is Mefter; fo that if it appears that the orthography of this word was fluctuating and variable, and depended on the habits of the different perfons who ufed it, no pofitive objection againft any fpecific mode of fpelling

it

it, is at all fair or well grounded. Mr. Malone
likewife remarks on the fpelling of chambelayne,
and objects to the omiffion of the letter r, obferving at the fame time, that if the queen had
omitted any letter it would have been the *m*. I
reply to this, that he ought to have known that
the word was derived from the French *chambelan*,
and therefore that the letter m could not have
been omitted, as there was no r in the French
orthography. Befides might not the r have been
omitted by accident? As to his exception alfo
to the fpelling of *Londonne*, which he fays was
never fo fpelt, I refer him to Elizabeth's Progrefs,
p. 231, vol. 2, where the orthography ftands
as in the letter *Londonne*: But there is another
objection, and that it feems is a fatal one, to
the unfortunate fpelling of *Hamptowne*. Is it to
be fuppofed, fays Mr. Malone, that this learned
queen who knew eight languages, fhould be fuch a
dolt as not to know the orthography of a word fo
familiar to her? But, I would afk, whether a man
pretending like Mr. Malone, to be fo converfant in
thefe matters, does not in fome fort anfwer to the
defcription of *dolt*? Who has not obferved the infinite licence of orthography, which characterifed
our language at this period? Who has not remarked, I do not fay, the numerous deformities, but
the capricious diverfity of fpelling in almoft every

book

book of the time? For a ftriking illuftration of the licentioufnefs of Englifh orthography at that period, I refer to a letter (in the Courtiers Academy printed in 1557), written by the learned Sir John Cheeke, to his loving friend Mafter Thomas Hoby.

In the preface to Upton's Fairy Queen, is the following remark on this fubject, as far as concerns the orthography of manufcripts. " The truth is, " that the printers and correctors of the prefs, " thought themfelves much wifer in this kind of " lore, than either the poet or his editors." See alfo Mafon's recent publication of Occleeve's Poems, from a MS bought by him at Leigh and Sotheby's, in which the editor remarks in his preface, p. 17 and 18. " That there is a degree " of uncertainty in all that can be faid about afcer- " taining the ftate of our language at former pe- " riods."

Rowe on this fubject fays, in his account of the life, &c. of Wm. Shakfpeare,—that " we are " to confider him as a man that lived in a ftate of " almoft univerfal licence and ignorance, there was " no eftablifhed judge, but every one took the " liberty to write according to the dictates of his " own fancy, &c. &c.

For a peculiar and indefinite manner of fpelling, I refer the reader to Queen Elizabeth's Progrefs
by

by Nicols, where in almost every page my observations will be amply corroborated ; he produces
inftances in which the fame word has eight different modes of orthography. In his note, p. 71, the
word court is fpelt in the following different modes,
corte, court, coorte, courte, courght. With regard to Hamptowne, it is very fingular, notwithftanding the pofitive manner in which Mr. Malone
afferted that it was uniformly fpelt Hampton, that
he himfelf has given an inftance of *Hamptown,*
befides, which I have myfelf feen, Wintown,
Cranftown, Hoptown, and Milfingtown ; and it
would be very extraordinary if the final e, fhould
in this word be repugnant to the analogy of the
language, when it forms the final letter of many
hundreds of names of places after the fyllable *ton.*

But we are now come to a mifnomer, compared
with which all the others it feems are trivial, that
is, the fpelling of Leycefterre, for Leycefter.
Then, to fhew how fairly and legibly that nobleman always wrote his name, we are referred to
the fac-fimile of his autograph, given us by Mr.
Malone ; but furely he would not wifh us to conclude, that all the autographs of the fame individual
will neceffarily be equally fair and legible. Are
the various autographs, for inftance, in the Britifh
Mufeum, all of them equally fair and legible?
and if one fpecific autograph be lefs legible than
the

the other, who will infer that it is therefore a forgery? Yet Mr. Malone is completely ignorant of the mode of fpelling the name at the period with which we are concerned. In page 72, he fays, that the true orthography is Leycefter; in the fame page he repeats more pofitively ftill, that " this nobleman himfelf always wrote it " Leycefter;" again he fays, in the fame page, that " he uniformly wrote it Leycefter." In direct refutation of thefe pofitive and dogmatical affertions, let me refer to the privy council book of that period, from which the following extracts are made, and by which it appears, that from January 19, to May 5, the name is not once fpelt Leycefter as Mr. Malone ftates.

19 January, 1586, E. of *Leicefter*, prefent in council.

21 January, ditto.

22 January, ditto, and fo on always the fame fpelling.

1 April,   1587, E. of *Leyceftre*, prefent.
Same day,   E. of *Leicefter*.
22 April, 1587, E. of *Leiceftre*, prefent.
23 April, 1587, E. of *Leyceftre*, prefent.
25 April, 1587, E. of *Leicefter*, prefent.
Same day,   E. of *Leiceftre*, prefent.
26 April, 1587, E. of *Leiceftre*, prefent.
Same day,   E. of *Leicefter*, prefent.

5 May,

5 May, 1587, E. of *Leycefter*, prefent.
18 June, 1587, E. of *Leicefter*, prefent.

Having brought forward fo many MS proofs,
I fhall now refer the reader to Burleigh's State Papers, p. 527, where it is fpelled *Lecefter*, in the
fame work, p. 543, it ftands *Leiceftre*, p. 545, it
is *Leceftre*; in the Annals of Elizabeth's Reign,
publifhed 1625, it is invariably printed Leicefter.
To fhew that it was not ufual in thofe times to
fpell thefe names with ftrict uniformity, in Burleigh's Papers, p. 543, *Northfolck*, ftands for Norfolk; in the fame page *Norfolck*, and in the following
page Norfolk, as it is ufed at this day. In p. 546,
of the fame book, Lord Shrewfbury's name is
fpelt *Scherufbereis*; In p. 560, he is addreffed by
the queen as lieutenant in her own hand, Therle
of *Shrewfbery*. It would be an endlefs, and a very
unedifying labour, to point out thefe varieties.
It is fufficient to have cited thefe inftances, to
fhew that Mr. Malone is utterly ignorant of the
matters, on which he fpeaks with fo much prefumption and arrogance.

From the difcuffion of this curious topic which
I have juft clofed, it will be remarked, how unfettled and capricious the orthography of our
language was at the period alluded to. The fpecimens I have quoted, will demonftrate the abfurdity

D   of

of fpeaking in a tone of decifion on thefe fubjects, or of drawing general inferences from fpecific inftances.

But we are now come to confider Mr. Malone's exceptions to the *Language* and *Phrafeology* of the MSS. The firft peculiarity, which he notices, is the word *pretty*, which he fays was not the phrafe of the time. Here we have only an affertion, which like the others, that Mr. Malone's book overflows with, is of the fame fallacious, and feeble nature. The word pretty was in general ufe, at this period, and is ufed by all the writers, who were cotemporary with Shakfpeare, as well as by Shakfpeare himfelf.

" For to a *pretty* ear fhe tunes her tale."
Venus, and Adonis.

" He that hath feen the fweet Arcadian boy,
  " Wiping the purple from his forced wound;
" His *prettie* tears betokening his annoy,
  " His fighs, his cries, his falling on the ground."
Thomas Lodge's Scillas Metam. 1589.

" An yvorie fhadow'd front, wherein was wrapped
" Thofe *prettie* boures, where graces couched lie."
Ibid.

" No

" No more my glances play with him fo *pretie*."
Ibid.

" Too traiterous *pretie* for a lover's *vieu*."
Ibid.

" Whofe *pretie* tops with five fweet rofes ends."
Ibid.

" That of their teares, there grew a *pretie* brook."
Ibid.

" Some *pretie* witneffe to the ftanders by."
Ibid.

" Delicious fhine her *pretie* eyes."
Ibid.

" *Pretty* wit."
As you like it.

A *Prety* and Pleafant Poeme of a whole Game of Chefs, is the title of a book printed in 1597.

After thefe inftances, efpecially as he allows Shakfpeare, and Ralegh to have ufed *pretty tales*, can this critic doubt whether the epithet was applied to written compofitions?

Thefe references muft be more than are ftrictly neceffary to overthrow Mr. Malone's exception.

But he like some unskilful horseman, it should seem, is prepared for a fall, and has provided against it. " I enter my protest" says he, " against the triumph of those, who may produce " antient examples of the usage of words to " which I object." This is curious. He attempts to prove the spuriousness of the MSS, by shewing that the words used in them, were not the words or phrase of the period to which the papers are attributed. Yet he enters his protest against every argument that upholds the opposite position. An ingenious mode of logic truly, and one that is calculated to save a world of argument on every subject to which it is applied. But let us hear his own justification of it. " If " says he, " out of four objections, only one should be " found incontrovertible, it will establish the spu- " riousness of the piece as well as four hundred." Surely it cannot be expected that a serious answer can be given to such a gross, and palpable absurdity; especially where it has been shewn to be impossible, that any reliance can be placed upon any such objections. A crown lawyer who on a case of high treason, after calling a list of witnesses in support of the charge, all of whom had been proved contradictory, and incompetent, would surely be extremely ridiculed if he were to exclaim; that if one witness could be produced whose evidence

could

could not be difproved, the contradictions, and perjuries of the others were to have no weight at all with the jury.

Then our critic proceeds to ftart objections againft the words *complement*, and *excellence*. With regard to the former, he objects to its ufe as a verb active, which he fays " was never known in " this fenfe, in that age, nor for fome time after- " wards." In refutation of this, I would refer the reader to Florio's Italian Dictionaty, 1611, where it is plainly ufed as a verb active; *complementare to complement*, and *compire* to ufe *complements*, or *ceremonies*.

Mr. Malone obferves on this topic, that till fome inftance be produced againft him he has a right to affume that it did not exift. I have here adduced a decifive evidence of its exiftence. By the fame right, and on the fame principle the public are threatened with an edition of Shakfpeare in *twenty volumes*, where perhaps, after filling up whole pages with ufelefs references as he has done here, it will end in an avowal of his ignorance, and the text will be left to fome plain and unfophifticated underftanding to reftore what has been defaced by the prefumptuous ignorance, and unfeeling drudgery of the commentator.

Now for the word *excellence*. Mr. Malone de - nies that it fignified the purity or goodnefs of

written compofitions.. But if the reader will turn
to Barrett's Alvearie, 1580, and to Florio already
quoted, he will fee that the word is unqueftionably,
ufed in the fenfe to which he objects; and furely
if the epithet has this fignification, it is the height
of abfurdity to fuppofe that it might not be applied
to written compofitions, as well as to any other
fubftantive to which adjectives are ufually applied:
I will however produce another inftance in the fecond fong in Brown's Paftorals, where he fpeaks
decidedly of the *excellence of art.*

In the Overthrow of Stage Plays in 1600, p.
25, we are told that " Nero being tickled with
" defire of prayfe, and loving to heare men ap-
" prove his playing on the ftage with clapping of
" their hands and crying out *excellent. excellent!*"

Two months after the publication of Mr. Malone's mafs of *hyper-criticifm,* he corrects himfelf
in the Gentleman's Magazine, as to the word *excellence;* and declares that " he had, had reafon fince
" to believe that the word was thus ufed in Shak-
" fpeare's time." It is furely a fingular circumftance, that the critic after afferting in the moft
decifive tone that the word was not ufed in the
above fenfe, fhould without any apology or confeffion of his own rafhnefs, retract his affertion. It
puts us in mind of the gentleman mentioned in the
Spectator,

Spectator, who knocked a man down in the ftreet, and then very civily begged his pardon.

The next objection is to the word *ourefelfe*. He fays that when ufed with the perfonal pronouns or prenominal adjectives, it was always written feparately. I fhall cite inftances as ufual to refute the objection. *Ourfelfe.* Henry VIII.'s preface to his own facraments printed by Bartelet, 1354, p. 2, and 93. Himfelf. Argument to the firft edition of Shakfpeare's Rape of Lucrece, 1594. In R. Whiteford's Worke for Houfeholders, 1530, " hide, and give moft diligence to order *yourefelfe* " and all youres, &c. that goth *before.*" *Myfelfe,* Venus, and Adonis, 1600, See Supplement to Johnfon, and Stevens edition. *Thyfelf*, twice written in ditto, p. 441, ditto. *Themfelves,* ditto, p. 411. *Itfelf*, Sonnets, p. 95. In Chriftopher Middleton's Hiftorie of Heaven, 1596, we find " for proofe whereof he fees how greate beafts " bow and humbly caft *themfelves* at wife mens " feet."

" Then thinkes he unto *himfelfe,* &c." *Hymfelfe.* See Barclay's Batayle of Jugurth, 32 B.

But Mr. Malone wifhes a diftinction to be drawn between manufcripts, and printed books, and obferves that the united words of *ourfelfe* is not to be found in the manufcripts of the age. In reply, I obferve that from the various citations

I have

I have made from printed books, it may very eafily be inferred, that they were joined in the manufcripts, from which the books were printed. For
though in a few inftances, whether from the care-
leffnefs of the compofitor, or any other caufe, the
printed copy might differ from the MS, yet it is
hardly poffible to fuppofe that this deviation would
take place in the various books I have juft inftanced.

What follows in the catalogue of Mr. Malone's objections, is the exception he is pleafed to
take againft the word *amuze*, which in its prefent fenfe, he fays is perfectly modern. In fupport of this exception, he refers us as ufual, to his
old friends, the dictionaries ; among which he
feems to have made many very elaborate refearches. Then he *amufes* us with a lift of names,
fuch as Barret, Cotrave, Bullekar, and Sherrwood,
in none of whofe works he has been able to find
the controverted word ufed in the fenfe to which
it is now applied. By fome fingular fatality in
the critical labors of Mr. Malone, he feems always
to look in the wrong place, for that, which perhaps
when he looks after, he wifhes not to find.
For had he turned to Florio's Italian Dictionary,
which I have before had occafion to quote, he
would have feen the word with the very fenfe an-
nexd to it, which he fo pofitively fays did not be-

long

long to it at that time. " To *amuse, trattenere,
tener a bada.*

Before I clofe this topic, I cannot refrain from
indulging myfelf in a fingle remark, on the habit fo
peculiar to Mr. Malone, of citing dictionaries
and lexicons in fupport of his objections. He
feems to have paid more devotion to Barret,
Cotgrave, Cawdrey, Bullokar, Sherwood, Cock-
ram, Philips, Cole, and Kerfy, than to the Nine
Mufes : and he looks on their works as authorities,
from which no appeal can pคffibly be had. But it
requires little reflection to know that thefe authorities are at beft defective; they cannot contain
all the varieties and obliquities of language. Of
fome, the works were profeffedly confined and par-
tial; and others brought to the tafk, fcanty and imperfect materials. The beft dictionary does not
contain all the words in ordinary and vernacular
ufe; and fo vaft is the extent of human diction,
and fo inadequate is the induftry of man to traverfe
the whole field of language, that the moft fagacious of them all have complained, that their labour is frequently circumfcribed, and their pur-
pofes perpetually defeated. Mr. Herbert Croft
fays, that Dr. Johnfon, who is the beft lexicogra-
pher the age has produced, has omitted thoufands
of words, not merely of different fignifications. I
have made this obfervation to fhew, that if Mr.

E   Malone

Malone is fuccefsful when he refers to dictionaries in fupport of his objections to the ufe of words, the authority on which he attempts to refute is fometimes queftionable, and always imperfect. But I have done more than this. I have fhewn even from the dictionaries, to which he is fo fond of appealing, that the words he excepts againft, are uniformly ufed in the very fenfe which he denies them.

We are now to confider, what our critic calls the incongruous circumftances attending the letter, the fuperfcription, the negative date, &c. Firft he objects to the fuperfcription. "For Mafter "Wm. Shakfpeare atte the Globe by Thames." "So that" he fays, in a ftyle of banter, "the "meffenger was to find out on which fide of the "Thames, north, or fouth, the theatre lay." Surely there is fomething too frivolous in this objection to be noticed with ferioufnefs ; for was it at all more neceffary that the fuperfcription of her majefty's letter fhould minutely point out the fide of the Thames to which it was directed, than that a letter to David Garrick, fhould have been fuperfcribed to Drury Lane Theatre on the eaft fide of Brydges Street. With regard to the negative date of this letter, though I can pofitively affert that there never was a date upon it, as has been malicioufly infinuated, it is only from conjecture that I afcribe

to

to it, that of 1588. It has alfo been infinuated that Lord Leicefter was dead, when this letter was written. It will be obferved however, that this is mere conjecture. I have alfo my conjectures on the fubject. The public will judge which is the moft probable. In 1587, Lord Leicefter went out a fecond time to the Low Countries, for the purpofe of raifing the fiege which was then carrying on againft Sluys. He returned it is well known, in difgrace with the privy council, on account of the mifcarriage of his enterprize. But a fhort time after he was reftored to the favour of her majefty. In July 1588, when the Armada arrived in the channel, Leicefter was appointed general at Tilbury fort, commanding 1000 horfe, and 22000 foot. After various engagements from 12th July, to 31ft of the fame month, the Armada was difperfed and purfued by the Englifh. Soon after this defeat, the queen went to St Paul's in public proceffion; and general thankfgivings were offered up in commemoration of that glorious event; and there is every reafon to conclude, that fhe was not inattentive at that period to her favorite amufement, theatrical exhibitions.

If any authority is allowed to the memoirs of Robert Cary, E. of Monmouth, in Nicol's Elizabeth's Progrefs, it feems " that plays, mafques, and " tournaments were fmall branches of thofe many

E 2   " fpreading

" fpreading allurements, which Elizabeth made
" ufe of to draw to herfelf the affections, and ad-
" miration of her fubjects. She appeared at them
" with dignity, eafe, grace, and affability." Now
from every authority it appears, that the Earl of
Leicefter, from that time July 31ft, was in perfect
health, and continued fo to the period of his death,
which, according to D'Arcey in his Hiftory and
Annals of Queen Elizabeth, happened on the
14th of December, 1588. Stowe's Cronicle however, publifhed in the year 1590, fays, " on the 4th
" of September, 1588, deceafed Robert Dudley,
" Earl of Leycefter, Lord Steward of her Majefty's
" Houfehold, &c. &c. at Cornbury in Oxford-
" fhire, from whence he was conveyed to his caf-
" tle at Kenilworth, and from thence to Warwick,
" where he was honorably interred." Admitting
therefore that he died on the 4th of September,
there was a fufficient interval of time, for his ufual
attendance on the Queen at theatrical reprefentations. Upon the hypothefis of the date 1588, a reference to Aggas's map of London in 1568, to
Vertue's map in 1560, and to that of Braun, and
Haugenburgius in 1573, proves nothing to the
purpofe. Yet I might refer to a map publifhed
by Mr Pennant in his Hiftory of London, which
is a copy of one publifhed in the year 1563. In
this map, there is to be feen on the Bank-fide, a
theatre,

theatre, which is fet down as " Shakfpeare's play-
" houfe." Now though this is evidently an anachronifm, (Shakfpeare not being born till 1564),
yet it appears that a theatre ftood which exactly
correfponds to the place, where the Globe Theatre
is fuppofed to have been built.

In order to corroborate his reafonings our critic ftates, that " he difcovered a contract made
" the 8th of January 1599-1600, between Philip
" Henflowe and Edward Alleyn the player, on the
" one part, and Peter Streete a carpenter on the
" other, for building the Fortune Play Houfe,
" near Golden Lane, which afcertained the di-
" menfions and plan of the Globe Theatre, there
" called the late erected Play Houfe on the Bank-
" fide, &c. &c. and I have lately difcovered" he
continues, " a bond executed by Burbage the
" player to this very Peter Streete, on the 22d
" Dec. 1593." So then, the whole reafoning
comprehended in this detail, is nothing more than
this! Peter Streete a carpenter, in 1599, entered
into a contract with Henflowe, and Alleyn, to
build the Fortune Play Houfe. It is afferted, that
this very carpenter in the year 1593, had executed
with Burbage of the Globe Theatre, a bond for
performance of covenants. It is likewife afferted,
that the articles of agreement referred to in this
bond, *probably* related to the building of the
Globe

Globe Theatre, and might fix the building of it at 1593 or 94. Now it is very obvious, *that* is, a reafoning *ex hypothefi*; which is equally the privilege of both parties on controverfies of this nature. Thefe articles of agreement might relate to any other concern in the life of Burbage, as well as to his connection with this theatre; or it might relate to the repairs of the theatre, or to any other tranfaction of the fame nature. But all that I wifh to fhew is, that amidft fuch a variety of conjectures, the conclufion of Mr. Malone, that " the Globe Theatre did not exift at the " time to which this letter muft be referred," is wholly unauthorized and unfounded

We have alfo fome curious objections to the ufe of the word *theatre*, on the grounds of its not being a word of the age. He fays that it fhould have been called the Globe Play Houfe, not the Globe Theatre. But I could produce innumerable illuftrations, to falfify this affertion, not only from his cotemporary writers, but even from Shakfpeare himfelf. In this inftance better authority indeed cannot be produced, than from Mr. Malone's Prologemena, vol. 2, p. 162, &c. where, in Stockwood's Sermon, publifhed 1578, cited in a note, on the fubject of the Curtain Theatre, it is faid " I know not how I might with the godly " learned, efpecially more difcommend the gor-
" geous

" geous playing-place erected in the fields, than
" to term it, as they are pleafed to call it a *The-*
" *atre.*" Again Mr. Malone fays in the fame page
of his Prologemena, that there were feven principal
Theatres, and four that were called " public
" *Theatres.*" We refer him likewife to his own
notes *Paffim* for the general ufe of the word.

" As in a *Theatre,* the eyes of men,
" After a well grac'd actor leaves the ftage,
" Are idly bent on him, that enters next,
" Thinking his prattle to be tedious, &c.

Richard 2d. A. 5. S. 2.

" This wide and univerfal *Theatre*
" Prefents more woeful pageants, &c.

As you like it.

So Mafter Reynold's anfwere unto Mafter D.
Reynolds, concerning *Theatre* fights, ftage playes,
&c. printed 1600. Again in the fame book,
Theatres, fights, and playes, p. 1, Lord Bacon
alfo ufes it in the difputed fenfe. " So as they all
" ftood up as in a *Theatre,* viewing this fight."

We are next told that the queen could not
poffibly have been at Hampton Court during the
holy-dayes, which were generally the times of
theatrical exhibitions. Thofe holidays are ftated
by

by Mr. Malone, to be Chriftmas, Twelfth-tide, Candlemas and Shrove-tide. But it might be afked, were there no holidays in Bartholomew-tide ? And is it unreafonable to fuppofe, that the queen gave orders for the acting of plays during that feftival, which was celebrated in the month of Auguft ?

Our critic proceeds to affert that the refidence of the queen is afcertained by the regifters of the privy council. Now, fays he, " From the " beginning of December, 1587, to the 8th July " 1588, fhe refided at Greenwich. On that day " fhe went to Richmond, where fhe remained to the " end of July." Now what appears from the Privy Council Books ? Allowing that fhe was at Greenwich on the 26th of December, 1587, fhe was at the Star Chamber, the 6th of February, 1588, on the 16th of April, fhe was at Hackney ; on the 14th of July, 1588, fhe was at Richmond ; and on July the 31ft, at St. James. Thefe ftatements which I have faithfully taken from the Privy Council books, wholly difprove the affertions of Mr. Malone. But his grand argument is, that during thefe periods, her majefty was not at Hampton. But furely, it cannot be denied, that the queen might have commanded plays to be acted at other times, as well as at the feftivals, enumerated by

Mr.

Mr. Malone, allowing for the fake of argument, his ftatements to be correctly made.

The next objection is, that the great poet, at the time to which this letter is referred, is fuppofed to be an eftablifhed actor, and the manager of a troop of actors. And then it is faid, " that his " firft excurfion to the metropolis could not have " been before 1586, or 1587." Granting this ftatement to be correct, it will be feen that he was now twenty-four years and a half old, being born in April 1564. Now what reafon is there to conclude from any thing that appears in the hiftory of his life, that at this age, his talents as an actor had not attracted the notice and received the patronage of his royal miftrefs? Then it feems our commentator has written an hiftory of the Englifh ftage, in the future edition of which it will be fhewn, that it is highly improbable that Shakfpeare fhould have produced a fingle drama, till fome time after the period of 1586. Granting this probability to be well founded, does it neceffarily follow, that he had not the management of the theatre at the time alluded to, or that he had not written the pretty verfes to Elizabeth, to which her majefty's letter refers?

But to fhew that our bard had not written any of his fublime productions at the above period, it is obferved, that none of his works are alluded to

F   by

by Nafhe, or Puttenham; the former of whom
was the author of an epiftle to the univerfities, in
which he reviews all the celebrated poets of the
time, and the latter of the art of poetry; and
that by neither of thefe writers, who publifhed in
the year 1589, is Shakfpeare at all referred to as
a dramatic poet. In reply to this, I obferve,
that no omiffion of this nature in the works of
cotemporary writers at all proves that Shakfpeare was not an author of reputation at that
time, becaufe there are many inftances in which
fimilar omiffions and equally remarkable may be
obferved; it is an extraordinary circumftance, that
Brown in his Britannia's Paftorals, publifhed 1613,
in the very zenith of Shakfpeare's reputation
as a dramatic poet, fhould have given a panegy-
rical enumeration of all the principal poets who
flourifhed about that time, fhould not have once
mentioned the very name of our immortal drama-
tift. He begins with Sydney, p. 36, folio edition;
then alludes to Chapman, with the eulogium of
" *learned Shepherd* ;" next Drayton, as a " *Second*
" *Ovid*;" Ben Johnfon, he characterifes thus,"

" Johnfon, *whom not Seneca, tranfcends his*
" *worth of praife.*"

" He likewife mentions Daniel, Brooke, Da-
vies, Withers, &c. &c.

But

But in this catalogue of poetical perfonages, the name of Shakfpeare is not once alluded to. It is no lefs extraordinary, that Sir William Temple, the moft accomplifhed writer of his age, in his enumeration of the epic poets of modern Europe, had entirely overlooked the immortal name of John Milton. In one word, no truth is more completely demonftrated to thofe who have made thefe refearches, than the fcantinefs and barrennefs of materials relative to the biography of Shakfpeare's time, and nothing feems to me a more convincing proof of it, than this circumftance; that after all the enquiries which have been directed to this fubject, we know fo little of Shakfpeare's theatrical life, that we are not even informed about the characters, in which he appeared on the ftage.

In a ftyle of banter, with which Mr. Malone is fometimes difpofed to diverfify, though it does not embeliifh, the ferious dullnefs of his work, that the note annexed by Shakfpeare to the letter in queftion, " is more like the punctilious exactnefs " of a merchant, or attorney, than the well known " negligence of the modeft and carelefs Shak- " fpeare." But the critic fhould have known, that this paper was in itfelf of a curious nature; that the moft negligent perfon, who had received a let-

ter

ter from his fovereign, would naturally treafure it up as a valuable token of royal condefcenfion, and as the moft flattering tribute, that could be paid to the genius of an author.

Of the fame nature is the remark, that it is improbable that the " *pretty verfes*," fhould have been loft, while the profe was fo carefully pre-ferved. The obfervation is fo very frivolous that it can fcarcely affect the queftion before us. But it is furely the very climax of folly, to form any conjectures concerning the lofs of papers, or their prefervation. Shakfpeare might pro-bably fet an higher value on the profe of his royal miftrefs, than on his own poetry; and the piece, which he addreffed to her, though expreffed in a complimentary ftyle, might be of fo flight a na-ture, that neither Shakfpeare himfelf, who was uniformly negligent of his poetical reputation, nor any of his cotemporaries, might think it neceffary to tranfmit it to pofterity. It is idle, however to frame conjectures concerning the prefervation, or lofs of papers, circumftances, which are governed by caufes of fuch various, and incidental opera-tions.

In a note Mr. Malone has favoured the readers of his work, with a fhort poem addreffed to Queen Elizabeth by Shakfpeare, in the mock-heroic ftyle. He has exhibited it in order to fhew the world,

that

that a critic can occafionally write verfes, as well as notes. But I fear, that the tendency, the meaning, and the conftruction of the lines, will perplex and baffle the ingenuity of all who may attempt to find either tendency, meaning, or conftruction in them. This is furely very gratuitous folly in the commentator. No one called for the difplay of poetical talent in a man, whofe province is as remote from poetry, as the notes which he fabricates, are foreign from the infpiration of the text he attempts to illuftrate. Why fhould he have leaped over the fence, which has hitherto fecured the facred ground of poetry, from the unhallowed intrufions of thofe, who labour in the humble, though ufeful departments affigned to compilers and commentators ?

" But," fays the critic " in the name which " has been exhibited as the hand-writing of the " queen, there are no lefs than fix grofs errors. Now reader, what is the firft error ? Why, " that " it is too fmall for the period, to which it muft " be referred." Here then we fee the wonderful art of the critic exhibited to perfection. At the diftance of two centuries he can afcertain the gage and dimenfions of a fignature ; and with a nice and accurate meafurement, fix the precife period at which it was written, by the fize and bulk of the letters. Mr. Malone is poffeffed of her

majefty's

majefty's autographs in the firft, fifth, tenth, and
fifteenth years of her reign; and it appears from
thefe, that her hand-writing gradually enlarged as
fhe advanced in life, and that in the year; 1587, or
1588, it was at leaft a fourth, perhaps a third
larger than when fhe came to the throne. God
fave the mark ! and could not this ingenious critic
by the fame rule, afcertain the fize of that of her
maids of honour, and ladies of her bed chamber,
and fix its progreffion, and dimenfions, as they advanced in life ? But to fpeak ferioufly. How is
it poffible to decide on the exact fize of a hand-
writing of any perfon, and by that fix the exact
period of his life at which it was written ?

The fecond error, it that the autograph inclines
fideways, whereas the genuine autograph is *bolt
upright*. Here the critic again reforts to his wonderful rule for meafuring her majefty's autograghs.
Now it happens unfortunately, that Mr. Malone's
fpecimens of the autographs are not *bolt upright*.
and, if as he remarks, the flourifh is always obferved
under the firft letter, in order to make a complete
E, how comes it, that in the Mufeum Vefpafian,
P, there is a letter from the queen with her fignature, of which the flourifh does not interfect the
letter, and leaves it therefore as complete an F as
in the fac-fimile of the Shakfpeare MSS. I have
in my poffeffion eight unqueftionable autographs of
this

this princefs, to official papers, in which this flourifh uniformly interfects the firft letter. I mention
this circumftance merely to fhew, that as it is fo
notorious that fhe was accuftomed to write her
name in the method alluded to, that if the imputed
forger had followed any model, (and how could he
have forged her name unlefs he did), that the par-
ticularity muft have neceffarily ftruck him.

Now we come to the fourth blunder, viz. in
the *a* of the autograph. I can fcarcely condefcend
to remark on an objection which is fo minute and
frivolous, that it almoft implies a degradation of
underftanding to have difcerned it. Let me quote
the paffage. " In the early part of her reign fhe
" formed the direct ftroke of that letter like other
" perfons: but by degrees it became higher than the
" circular part ; nor was it ever open or looped at
" the top, &c. &c. This oxquifite minutenefs of
remark, is highly amufing in our commentator ; it
reminds us of Malvolio, who was not in the leaft more
accurate in the difcovery of his lady's hand-writing.
" By my life this is my lady's hand : thefe be her
" very c's, her u's, and thus makes fhe her great
" P's ; it is in contempt of queftion, her hand."

Of the fame nature are the other objections
which follow, relative to the b of her majefty's
hand. The argument has nothing in it that makes
an appeal to the tafte, curiofity, or judgment of the

reader

reader. I fhall difmifs it with a very little comment. I would, however, afk how any critic can afcertain the precife form, in which an individual writes a name, or frames a word, and lay down a peremptory and determinate opinion upon fuch a fubject. He who writes his name at one time in one manner, will write it again in another; and I believe, that it is abfolutely impoffible, that the fame words, or letters fhould be framed in exact refemblance to each other, in the ordinary habits of writing. When we write our names, we do not make fac-fimiles from any preceding model : befides the whole weight of the objection, will overthrow the argument which Mr. Malone labors to eftablifh; for had the fpecimens exhibited in the Shakfpeare MSS, correfponded with fuch minutenefs, to the uniform, and well known fignatures of Queen Elizabeth, thefe would be *prima facie*, a prefumption of fraud. The queen never wrote her name at different times, in the fame form and modification of the letters. It is impoffible that fhe could. But if the autographs afcribed to her, fhould be found exactly in fize and form, to anfwer to any fpecific fpecimen of her fign manual, it would neceffarily give birth to a fufpicion of impofture and fabrication. I remember the trial of a difputed will, where in anfwer to a claim that was fet up, it was obferved

by

by the council, that the name in the will fo exactly correfponded to the known method in which
the deceafed wrote his name, that no further objection could be had to it. In reply to this, it was
very judicioufly remarked on the other fide, that
the very circumftance alledged to be in favor of
the will, was totally deftructive of it; inafmuch as
no perfon ever wrote his name twice exactly in the
fame way. In fupport of this remark, a perfon in
court was defired to write his own name feveral
times on a fheet of paper, which he did, and on
prefenting it to the bench, the deviation was fo
very obvious, that the will was entirely fet afide
upon the very grounds, which appeared fo incon-
teftably in its favour.

But before I clofe this part of the fubject, I
will juft advert to the alphabet adduced by Mr.
Malone in his firft plate. Now in this very
alphabet it is obfervable that the letters deviate
materially from the two extracts made from the
Cotton MSS, in the Mufeum. In the fame extracts the letters differ from each other; particularly the letter (t), in which there are no fewer
than five obvious deviations. The extracts alfo differ from the letter of the queen in the Herald's College, nor do they differ lefs from one written by
her, before fhe came to the throne, in the Mufeum.
See Vefpafian, f. 3. p. 20. I would here admonifh

G   Mr.

Mr. Malone, when he publifhes any future fac-fimiles, to be more correct in copying from the
originals before him ; becaufe the flighteft infpection will convince any one who compares them,
that he has been intentionally incorrect in the fac-
fimile he has publifhed.

Our critic, it muft be obferved in exhibiting
thefe comparifons, takes it for granted that the
fpecimens he difplays are genuine. But I have
reafon to entertain doubts concerning their authenticity. When I infpected thefe papers in the
Mufeum, in the prefence of a gentleman univer-
fally allowed to be a competent judge of thefe
matters, we urged an objection before two other
official gentleman who verfed as they may be fuppofed to be therein, were not at that time able to
anfwer. The objection was, that the letter N beginning, " I thanke you good Harry," &c. &c.
difcovered a reverfe, or an impreffion on the blank
page oppofite to it againft which it was fol-
ded, of the whole body of the letter, as well as
the queen's fignature. This appearance, certainly
a very extraordinary one to be produced by common ink, is not only obfervable in the body of the
letter, which was prepared by a clerk, but alfo in
the fignature ; fo that if this is to be confidered
as a genuine inftrument it is evident, her majefty
and the fecretary or clerk muft have ufed the fame

ink ;

ink ; which is not very eafy to fuppofe, even if
the ink were fuch, as was ever known to be in
common ufe. Another objection to the opinions
of Mr. Malone, as to the authenticity of thefe
papers, is, the circumftance of the letters being
placed in a collection of a totally different nature,
and called " The Book of Border Matters till the
" year 1583." The laft objection is, (and it is
a material one), that there is written in one of the
leaves, " *One of the bundles I bought of Mr. Phil-*
" *lips.*" Who this Mr. Phillips was, probably
we fhall be informed by Mr. Malone, upon fome
future occafion. Perhaps he was one of the
friends, who correfponded on matters of antiquity
with Sir Hans Sloane, and received from his cre-
dulous employer, commiffions fimiliar to thofe alluded to in an ingenious epiftle, addreffed fome
years ago to that great antiquary.

An Epiftolary Letter to Sir Hans Sloane.

Since you, dear doctor fav'd my life
To blefs by turns & plague my wife,
In confcience I'm oblig'd to do,
Whatever is enjoin'd by you :
According to your own command,
That I fhould fearch the weftern land,
For curious things of every kind,
And fend you all that I could find.

G 2

I've

I've ravag'd air, earth, fea, and caverns,
Men, women, children, town, and taverns,
And greater rarities can fhew,
Then Grefham's College ever knew;
Which carrier Dick fhall bring you down,
Next time his waggon comes to town.

First then obferve, and you fhall fee
A very, very rarity;
It is the true authentic fcore,
On which King David us'd to pore,
And gain'd fuch wond'rous approbation,
He was firft fiddle of the nation.

I've got three drops of that fame fhower,
Which Jove in Danaës lap did pour,
From Carthage brought, the fword I'll fend,
Which brought Queen Dido to her end.
The ftone whereby Goliah died,
Which cures the head-ach, well applied.
The fnake-fkin, which you may believe,
The devil caft, who tempted eve.
A fig leaf apron, 'tis the fame,
That Adam wore to hide his fhame,
But now wants darning; I've befide
The blow by which poor Abel died;
A whetftone worn exceeding fmall,
Time us'd to whet his fcythe withal.
The pigeon ftuff'd, which Noah fent
To tell him when the waters went.
A feather from the honeft raven,
That brought Elijah fcraps from heav'n.
A bull-rufh taken from the cradle,
In which young Mofes us'd to paddle.

Sr.

St. Dunſtan's tongs, which ſtory ſhews,
Did pinch the devil by the noſe.
With a knife-point full of that ſalt,
Lot's wife was turn'd to, for the fault,
Which ſince is grown ſo very common,
Who has it not, cannot be woman.
The very ſhaft, which all may ſee,
That Cupid ſhot at Anthony;
And which above the reſt I prize,
A glance of Cleopatra's eyes.
Fringe work compos'd of thoſe rich threads,
Broke at the loſs of maidenheads;
Rare, curious things, by Leiceſter ſeen,
And ſhewn him by a virgin-queen;
At leaſt to him or Howard ſhewn,
Things never heard of ——
Some ſtrains of eloquence, which hung
In Roman times, on Tully's tongue;
Which lay conceal'd, and loſt had been,
But Cowper found them out again;
A goad which nightly us'd will prove,
A certain remedy for love.
As Moore cures worms in ſtomachs bred,
I've pills cure maggots in the head,
With the receipt too, how to make 'em,
To you I'll leave the time to take 'em.
I've got a ray of Phœbus ſhine,
Found in the bottom of a mine.
A lawyer's conſcience, large and fair,
Fit for a judge himſelf to wear.
I've a choice noſtrum, fit to make
An oath a church-man will not take;

In

In a thumb-phial you fhall fee,
Clofe cork'd fome drops of honefty ;
Which after fearching kingdoms round
At lalt were in a cottage found ;
An antidote, if fuch there be,
Againft the charms of flattery.
I han't collected any care,
Of that, there's plenty ev'ry where ;
But after wond'rous labor fpent,
I've got one grain of rich content.
It is my wifh, it is my glory,
To furnifh your nick-nackatory ;
I only beg, whene'er you fhew 'em,
You'll tell your friends, to whom you owe 'em ;
Which may your other patients teach,
To do, as has done.

Yours,

T. H. (edges.)

We now return to the critic, whofe next topic
relates to " EXTRACTS FROM MISCELLANEOUS
" PAPERS, A NOTE OF HAND, AND A RECEIPT."
Under this head we have a moft curious difquifition concerning the fpelling of the poet's name.
" The fabricator of thefe papers is faid to have
" been led into his miftake by *Mr. Steevens, and*
" *Myfelf.*" Then we have a long and as ufual a very
tedious ftory about this miftake ; *how* in the year
1776, *Mr. Steevens, and Myfelf* traced the three
fignatures in the will ; *how* two of them appeared

Shakfpere,

Shakſpere, but a third appeared to have an *a* in the ſecond ſyllable. " *Accordingly we have ſo exhibited* " *the poet's name ever ſince.* I had no ſuſ- " picion," ſays the critic, " of my miſtake, till " about three years ago, &c." From this ſtate- ment, it ſeems that theſe ſtupendous critics re- poſed on this error for near twenty years, till after having deluded the public during that period, and receiving the hint from another perſon, one of them reſolves to examine the original (which he might and ought to have done before) again, and this enquiry putting it once more into his brain, to aſcertain his error, *if any error there was,* rela- tive to the name, before he publiſhed his new edition of Shakſpeare.

Then the commentator, on an inſpection of ſome papers, recently diſcovered by Mr. Albany Wallis, appears to have rectified his miſtake, and allows that the name ſhould be ſpelled Shakſpere. Yet notwithſtanding his having ſet himſelf right in his miſtake, with an inſtinctive predilection for his own blunder, he continues to write it *Shakſpeare.* Why he does ſo, will appear for reaſons aſſigned in " *My life of him.*" Still " harping upon my " daughter," the *Twenty volumes royal octavo.* Upon the whole it muſt appear that the manner of Shakſpeare's ſpelling his own name reſts only on grounds of probability. For when we conſider,

as

as I have more than once been obliged to remark, the extreme licence which at this period, and for some time after prevailed in the orthographies both of MSS, and of printed copies; it is fcarcely poffible to pronounce upon this fubject. In proof of this, I refer the reader to his will in the Prerogative Office, in the body of which it will be feen that his name is thus fpelt *Shack-fpeare.* But furely it is the moft provoking effrontery to affert, that the neceffary confequence of his having three or four years before his death, written his own name *Shak-fpere,* is a certain proof of the forgeries of the papers; when we know that during his life, his cotemporaries always fpelt his name Shakefpeare, and that he himfelf from the year 1594, till his deceafe, ufed the fame orthography in each of the various editions of his Lucrece, and his Venus and Adonis. But continues our Critic, " whether " I am right or wrong, it is manifeft that he " himfelf wrote it Shakfpere :" yet let us hear the conclufion : The conclufion is, that thofe papers in which a different orthography appears, muft be forgeries. I anfwer that the papers are not forgeries, becaufe the orthography in this refpect is different. The reafon why Mr. Malone himfelf, maintains his former fpelling, is that there is no

original

original Manufcript letter, of his name. If therefore there is this incertitude concerning the name,
who can put his finger on any fpecific fpelling of
it and fay that is not the genuine one ? I may fay,
in the fame words which Mr. Malone has ufed,
in juftification of his own fpelling, that when any
original letter or MS of Shakfpeare's fhall ever be
difcovered, then and not till then, will the orthography in my MSS be difproved.

In p. 121, Mr. Malone fays, that his engraver
defired him to furnifh him with an archetype for one
of the concluding letters, viz. (r): and that he
inadvertently took down the firft MS that came to
hand, and pointed out to him a German (r). Here
we fee, that Mr. Malone himfelf can be occafionally guilty of interpolation, though he has fo
thorough an abhorrence of Forgers; he takes
down an old German MS, in order to furnifh a
fac-fimile of Shakfpeare's hand-writing!! Now
with regard to the ufe of the Chancery r in the
Shakfpeare MSS of which he complains; he
fays, " that now and then, a fignature may be
" found in which it occurs ; but in the ordinary
" or fecretary hand I have never met with it."
He has never met with it. This is admirable !
And how is the reader to eftimate this fort of reafoning? Every one who has examined the topics,
on which I have been fpeaking, muft have had

H   abundant

abundant proof of the flender claims which this critic has to a blind confidence in his own opinions, and affertions.

For the long or chancery r, *as he has never met with it*, I refer him to Wright's Court-hand, Reftored, (a book, the authority of which cannot be doubted) there he will find that this objectionable letter has been in conftant ufe fince Henry the fourth's time, as by reference to many records of more antient date, it will appear to have been for many centuries previous to that period.

It is very curious, that in p. 250, he tells us, that Lowine the player, never had his name exhibited with *ine*, as the final letters. But the proof of this! Why, " *he never met with it.*" Of the critical accumulations of this gentleman in his intended life of Shakfpeare, I know nothing at prefent, but from what he has intimated to the public, concerning them, I hope that he will not follow his old and favorite mode of reafoning, in concluding things not to be in exiftence which he himfelf *has not met with*. On this head, I fhall content myfelf with afferting, that I have met with (what he ought to have feen) the name of *Lowine* in the lift of actors, prefixed to the firft folio edition of the immortal breathings of that mufe, who is about so be mangled and lacerated, in twenty ponponderous

derous volumes, fo fully announced by the inde-
fatigable compiler.

I might refer the reader to the different variations in the fac-fimiles, which the critic himfelf
has exhibited ; were I not confcious, that the
labor of following Mr. Malone through the
long labyrinth of abfurdity, in which he involves
himfelf and his reader, muft have been already
intolerable and difgufting. But what does the
whole argument amount to ? Why, it proves
that taking for granted, that thefe papers are
forgeries; Mr. Malone's blunders were in fact
the fources, from which they were derived.
What muft the world think of a man, fhould it
appear by fome hidden evidence now in the womb
of time, that the whole mafs of papers was an
impofture, when it is his own confeffion, that the
moft prominent features of it were derived from
his errors ?

With the fame mifcrofpic powers of criticifm,
our objector obferves, that Shakfpeare " when in
" health wrote a fmall hand, as was the general
" mode at that time, and that this is not the cafe
" with the forged MSS." What proof does Mr.
Malone adduce ? Where is it manifeft that he
wrote this fmall hand ? For, that he did not write
in that way, is unqueftionably proved by his autographs to the will, and to thofe which are now in

H 2   Mr.

Mr. Wallis's poſſeſſion, the only genuine ſpecimens he admits that are to be found.

We are told, that in the *projeĉted* HISTORY
OF THE STAGE, the critic has aſcertained the payment of a play at court, and that the ſum paid for
each repreſentation there, in the reign of Elizabeth,
was no more than ten pounds. He ſays, that he
has found this from authentic documents. To theſe
authentic documents, however, he has forgotten to
refer us. We muſt ſtill give him credit, for that
which in all diſcuſſions of this nature, muſt be held
an indiſpenſable duty; I mean, a reference to the
documents, on which an aſſertion reſts. Then
Mr. Malone points out the abſurdity of Lord Leiceſter's paying to the aĉtors thirty-one pounds more
than was charged to him. The weakneſs of this
ſpecies of objeĉtions, which are multiplied through
the whole work of our commentator, is very apparent. Was it an unuſual thing, at that period,
that a nobleman who lived in the magnificence
and ſplendor of Lord Leiceſter, ſhould pay for a
favorite amuſement, and to his favorite aĉtor, no
more, than the mere literal expences, that were
incurred?

But as another denotation of forgery, it is remarked, that the poet is repreſented in the MSS
to be ſo ignorant, as not to know an earl's proper
title: and then we are informed, that " your
" grace"

" grace" is the ufual mode of addrefs to dukes ;
but that the circumftance of its being applied to
Leicefter, is a proof of the papers being forged.
But it is worth while to obferve, that Mr. Malone
himfelf readily acknowledges, that the title was
not confined to dukes, but that it was applied indifcriminately to the king, and the princes of the
blood. Now it fhould feem from this very circumftance, that the mode of addrefs was not confined to dukes; and we well know, that it is neither
the appropriate title of king, or queen, nor of
the princes and princeffes of the blood ; your
majefty being the ftyle of the one, and their high-
neffes of the other. So, that here we have a proof
of the licence, and latitude of its application ; and
there is no reafon to conclude, that it never was
ufed to individuals of inferior rank, to the perfonages alluded to.

Befides Mr. Malone's argument is precifely
this ; that the *moft common* addrefs to peers of the
degree of dukes, being that of " your grace,"
it follows that Shakfpeare according to the MSS,
muft have been groffly ignorant of the ftyle, in
which noblemen were addreffed. Now, if ever
a conclufion was completely difclaimed by the premifes, it is this, which Mr. Malone has hazarded.
The very circumftance of, *your grace*, not being
generally fo applied, might probably be the reafon

of

of Shakfpeare's ufing it here. Had Shakfpeare been a courtier, and familiarized to the phrafe and accents of high rank, it was furely the moft innocent, and natural flattery he could ufe, to addrefs his patron in a ftyle, fuperior to that, which was literally appropriated to him. Or, if he was not habituated to the language of the court on thefe occafions (which as far as appears from his education, and life, is the moft probable hypothefis), it is more likely ftill, that he would ufe the language of flattery in his addrefs to Leicefter. It was natural for him to apply a title, in which if he erred, he erred on the fafe fide, and which the inherent weaknefs of our nature would rather approve, as the tribute of a zealous though incorrect obeifance, than the ill-placed compliments of untutored rufticity.

This hyper-critic now objects to a tranfaction in which Lowine is concerned which appears in the receipts of Shakfpeare. It ftates, that at the time this Mafter Lowine was rewarded " forre " his good fervyces, ande well playinge, he was " juft twelve years of age, and does not appear to " have joined the company till after the acceffion " of King James." But as ufual, Mr. Malone brings forward no proof, which unqueftionably afcertains the time of his joining the company, fo that no inference againft the MSS is to be drawn from what

he

he is pleafed to affert. That he might have at that time performed the part of Arthur in King John, or the Duke of York in Richard the third, will eafily be admitted; or that he might have occafionally taken female charaćters, which we know at that time were performed by young men. Befides it appears from the MSS, that only the fum of two fhillings is fet down for Mafter Lowine, a fum, very inadequate indeed to the fervices of an older performer, but which on the grounds of his extreme youth, was perhaps a fufficient falary.

We now come to the note of hand of *John Hemynge*, not *Hemynges*, as our fagacious commentator has it*.

    " One moneth from the date hereof, I doe
" promyfe to paye to my good and worthye freynd
" John Hemynge, the fum of five pounds and
" five fhillings, Englifh moneye, as a recompenfe
" for hys greate trouble, in fettling and doinge
" much for me at the Globe Theatre, as alfo for
" hys trouble in goinge downe for me to Statford.

    Witnefs my hand,   Wm. Shakfpere.
September the nynth, 1589.

* See Appendix to Malone, where *Heminges*, and *Hemynge*, occur in the fame deed and as the fame perfon.

On

On another paper is the following receipt, which is attached to the note of hand by three pieces of wax.

" Received of Mafter Wm. Shakfpeare, the " fum of five pounds and five fhillings, good En- " glifh money, thys nynth day of October, 1589.

"Jn°. Hemynge."

As to the fignature of the poet, differing in this note from the reft laid before the public, and for the " firft and laft time fpelt in his own genuine " manner;" I have it in my power to fhew many inftances, in which the name is fpelt in this mode, in feveral other papers which I have not publifhed; I have however, amply fhewn in a former part of this volume, the unfettled and indeterminate ftate of our old orthography; and the numerous variations, which at that time it admitted. With regard to the alledged difference of hand-writing in the fignatures, the fpecimens will be found with a very flight examination, to differ from each other, in the fame degree only as the fignature of the fame individual would at different times. And what ftrefs can properly be laid upon a point fo minute and frivolous as the accidental omiffion of the letter (r) in Stratford? Did Mr. Malone himfelf never omit a letter ih the hafte and negligence of writing?

But

But the obfervations, in which I fhall next follow him, are very extraordinary. "Need I "call your attention" fays the critic, to the "fum of five guineas, here in fact, though not in "words promifed to be paid?" Now let any one turn to the receipt, and fee how far the ftatement is true and correct in mere point of fact. Does it appear that the fum of five guineas is promifed to be paid? The accidental fum paid for the fpecified fervices being five pounds and five fhillings; who fhall fay, that the fum of five guineas is reprefented in the receipt? For inftance in the extract, Mr. Malone has given us, from the Royal Houfehold Eftablifhments, p. 255, the joiner's fee is fet down 19*l.* 19*s.* o*d.* and the record 16*l.* 16*s.* 8*d.* Will any one fay that the former of thefe fums reprefented nineteen guineas, and the other fixteen guineas and eight pence? Now unfortunately for the argument, it will appear from his own Prologomena, vol. 2, p. 254, in the account of monies received by Phil. Henflowe, that there is this ftatement

"26 of Defember, 1591,"
"*Received at the fege of London* iii*l.*: iii*s.*: o*d.*"

and were it not a fubject beneath attention, I make no doubt, that I could produce from antient records innumerable inftances of the fame nature;

I   equally

equally fenfelefs, and fatal to his own caufe, is the affertion, that xxi fhillings, or cv fhillings was the moft ufual mode of writing. Now the beft anfwer to this, will be to refer him to the Prolo-gomena, where it appears from the fame extracts, 1591, that the accounts were kept in pounds, fhillings, and pence. In fhort, it comparatively occurs in very few inftances, where the accounts kept in fhillings are above the number of xx.

A great emphafis is laid on the fac-fimile of Hemynge's hand-writing, which the moment he faw it, the critic inftinctively pronounced not to be genuine. Then we find him groping about the Prerogative Office, where he did not find what he looked for; though as I have before obferved from good authority, that had he been fuccefsful in his fearch, he could not have decyphered them. But we are informed, that to prove the *Hemynge* fhould have been *Heminges*; he was furnifhed from Mr. A. Wallis with a deed of John Heminges, dated Feb. 10, 1617-18, and of which he has given an autograph in plate 2, in which he has fagacioufly difcovered, that " there is no more fimilitude be-" tween the two fignatures, than Hebrew, or Chi-" nefe characters have to Englifh." And here let me requeft the reader to attend to this difcovery, and obferve the critic caught in his own net.

On Wednefday 30th of December 1795, Mr
Wallis,

Wallis, accompanied by Mr. Troward, requefted to fee me upon particular bufinefs. When they entered the room, Mr. Wallis apparently in a jocofe manner, and directing his hand to his pocket, exclaimed, " I have fomething here that " will deftroy the validity of your Shakfpeare " papers." He then produced the deed quoted by Mr. Malone, figned John Heminges, which I obferved was totally unlike the fignature of Hemynge, I had laid before the public. Mr. Wallis was then fhewn four receipts or memorandums, figned John Heminges, (which exactly correfponded with the hand-writing in his deed), one of which ftood in this form, dated in the year 1602-3.

" Hadde fromm Mafter Shakfpeare for ufe of " the Curtayne, the fomm of fortenn fhillings."

dated

Octobree 12, 1602.

Thefe four receipts are thus indorfed, " Payde " as hereinn mentyonedde, Wm. S." and are wrapped in another paper, on which is written " Receipts forre moneyes givenne toe mee bye " the *talle Heminge*, onne accounte o the Cur- " tayne Theatre."

Wm. S.

I 2   Among

Among thefe papers, there are at leaft twenty other memorandums, or difburfements of monies, in which this perfon, Heminges is always diftinguifhed as the *tall Heminges* of the Curtain Theatre, from the Hemynge I have laid before the world in my publication. Befides thefe documents I have the fame Heminges as a fubfcribing witnefs to feveral parchment deeds, with Shakfpeare and others. Now in confequence of Mr. Wallis having in his poffeffion the deed before mentioned, I was well aware, that it would be a high dainty to our critic, to have an opportunity of nibbling at the parchment ; I therefore, requefted that gentleman very earneftly, that Mr. Malone might be permitted to copy, or make any other ufe of this deed, that he might think proper. I was defirous alfo of putting fome deeds of my own into his hands, which I knew he would very willingly copy as proofs againft me ; but out of motives of mere compaffion, I defifted from my intention. Well, Mr. Wallis politely permitted him to take a copy of the deed, and in confequence, in Plate 2, No. 6, he has moft affuredly given the autograph with confiderable *fidelity*. It is amufing, therefore, to fee him like a whale rolling about in the depths of his own blunders : and entering into an elaborate proof to fhew that the s final was in common ufe at that time, to account for its being written *He-minges.*

minges. But this is another proof of his ignorance, of the orthography of proper names at that time, even as they were printed. Had he looked to the editor's dedication prefixed to the firft folios, he would have there found the name thus fpelled, without the s final *Heminge*. And fo indefinite was the orthography at that period, that in the lift of Actors in the fame vol. he is called *Heminges*. In p. 140 of Mr. Malone's work, he fays, that Heminge was married to Rebecca *Nuell*, widow. Now, as a proof that this ingenious gentleman cannot read, I would remark, that the original MS has it Rebecca Knell, widdow. Then in a ftyle of banter in which he is not very fuccefsful, he attacks poor Heminge with want of gallantry in leaving his wife to go down to Statford.

Are then the attachments of our amorous commentator fo clofely rivetted, that in the fecond year of his marriage, no urgency of bufinefs fhould divert him from the arms and the bed of his miftrefs, even for a few nights ? and with regard to his objection to the accidental ufe of Statford, I cannot help obferving the curious changes which he rings upon the objectionable authority, when in one fentence he finds fault with their being redundant, at another, with their being deficient in the letters. But, as he fays p. 132, " I will leave this

to

to be determined " by fome one better verfed in " decyphering nonfenfe, tn..n I am."

Mr. Malone now comes to an objection, on which by the affiftance of fome ingenious friend, he has been enabled very amply to expatiate. Very luckily, he fays, that he has difcovered the form of a promiffory note at that period, and as the note among the MSS does not conform in every refpect to it, he very fagacioufly concludes, that it was forged for the occafion. Let us obferve the fpecimen given by Mr. Malone.

Mem. " That I Gabrell Spencer the 5th of " Aprell have borrowed of Philippe Henflowe " the fum of thirtie fhellynges in redy money to " be payed unto him agayne, *when he fhall demande* " *yt.* I faye borrowed xxxs.
                                    " Gabrieel Spencer."

This is copied as Mr. Malone ftates, from Henflowe's MS Regifter.

Then he gives an inftance of a note or bill of debt, payable one month after date.

" The 1 and twentieth daye of Septtember, " a thoufand fix houndard, borrowed of Mr. " Henfhlowe in redii monie the fom of fortie
                                    " fhellings

" fhellings to be paid the twentie daie of October
" next folleinge the date herof, in witnefs herof,
" I fet to my hand.

" John Duke."

Another form was,—" Received 30 die Ja-
" nuarii 1598 of —— the fum of —— to bee re-
" payed unto him, or his affignes upon the laft of
" Febuary, next enfuinge, whereof I bind me, my
" heires, executors, and adminiftrators." None
of thefe it is faid, whether entered in the book
of the lender, or written on feparate flips of
paper, were indorfable over, nor could an action at law be maintained on them.

To this laft obfervation, I take no exception.
I do not contend that the memorandums in the
Shakfpeare MSS were legal or transferable fecurities. All I contend for is, that there can be no
decifive proof that this form of acknowledgement
of a debt, or a promife to repay it, might not
have been ufed at that time, notwithftanding
what is faid to difprove or invalidate it, either
by Mr. Malone himfelf, or by his ingenious
friend.

But the two authorities clafh with each other,
and according to all the rules of ftrict reafoning,

as well as of ftrict evidence, are mutually deftructive of the feveral proofs they adduce. In the
elaborate hiftory of promiffory notes, which is
thrown into the lumber of an appendix, inftead
of framing a connected fyftem of argument in his
text, it is laid down as a fort of axiom, that in the
period on which we are occupied, it was effential
to every inftrument of this kind, that it fhould
contain a claufe to exprefs the fealing of the paper.
For inftance. " In witnefs whereof I fet to my
" feale, &c." It is obfervable that this is alfo taken
from Henflowe's Regifter. Now in the bill of
debt, which Mr. Malone himfelf has exhibited,
there is no fuch claufe as this inferted, nor does it
appear that the inftrument was fealed by the party,
who was bound by it. Here then are two contradictory authorities. The ingenious friend fays
that every inftrument muft haye been fealed, and
that none exifted without it. The critic himfelf
produces a fpecimen, where there is no claufe relative to fealing at all; and what is very remarkable, both of them feem to have been exploring
the fame records; and each produces a fpecimen,
which falfifies and invalidates that of the other.

Mr. Malone from the nature of his objection,
appears to me entirely ignorant of the law, hiftory, and commerce, of the country. He does
not confider that the antient ufages of a bill or

promife

promife to pay, or to do any thing, becaufe there was by ftatute law, no definite and prefcribed form of writing them, on that very account, were by confequence uncertain and variable. He feems to fuppofe that the origin and ufe of notes was not prior to the ftatutes which made them negotiable, viz. the ftatutes 9th and 10th, William 3d, and 3d and 4th, Anne, c. 51. Thefe ftatutes firft made them negotiable, but it is reafonable to fuppofe that they were in exiftence before this period, as the 9th and 10th, William and Mary, c. 7, which, " is entitled an act for the better payment " of inland bills of exchange," prefcribes no fpecific form, but merely creates provifions to give them a legal negotiation and effect.

Without the aid of the dull reafoning in the appendix, I am ready to acknowledge, that the promiffory note did not exift legally at this period, and I am alfo ready to allow, that among merchants, it was not the ufual mode of giving fecurities, or of acknowledging debts. Among thofe, who were engaged in commerce, it is natural to fuppofe, that no inftrument would be in general ufe, but what was recognized by law. But the fame reafoning does not apply with equal force to tranfactions between individuals. It is ftated, that the want of thefe promiffory notes, &c. was very feverely felt in the mercantile world, and

K   the

the inconvenience of fealed obligations a confiderable matter of complaint. This inconvenience muft have been much more feverely experienced in the pecuniary intercourfes of thofe, who did not ftand in a mercantile relation to each other. By confequence therefore, fome mode of acknowledging the receipt of monies on one hand, or of promifing to pay them on the other, would naturally be reforted to, where a mutual confidence exifted. The notes &c. in the Shakfpeare MSS merely relate to a private tranfaction between two very intimate friends. The fums were fmall, and neither of the parties thought it neceffary to clothe their contracts in the inconvenient fhape of ftrict legal rules. This very often happens at the prefent moment. I have myfelf often feen the vowels I, O, U, with the fum of money annexed; and this has been the only acknowledgement between the parties, and that to a very confiderable amount. As thefe papers are not put into circulation, they are frequently kept in a defk or drawer, by way of a mere private memorandum.

Having difmiffed this topic, on which I truft that the remarks I have made, will be equally clear and fatisfactory, I now proceed to the letter to Anna Hatherway. Here Mr. Malone invokes Venus, her fon and all the loves, and the graces. The firft time I believe, fo ill-omened an

invo-

(75)

invocation was ever addreſſed to theſe perſonages.
Commentators, and critics are not in general the
ardent votaries, nor the favoured choice of the
beautiful divinity. Nor is it very uſual to invoke
the inſpiration of this goddeſs, to ſubjects of re-
condite and abſtruſe reſearches into black letter,
from whence the illuminations of genius, and taſte,
and ſcience are neceſſarily excluded. But leaving
this ridiculous topic, let us attend to the objections
the critic takes to the letter, I have alluded to.
The letter is as follows.

" Deareſte Anna

" As thou haſte alwaye founde mee toe mye
" worde moſte trewe ſoe thou ſhalt ſee I havee
" ſtryctlye kepte mye promyſe I pray you per-
" fume thys mye poore locke withe thye balmye
" kyſſes forre thenne indeede ſhalle kynges
" themmeſelves bowe ande paye homage toe itte.
" I doe aſſure thee no rude hande hathe knottedde
" itte thye Willy's alone hathe done the worke
" Neytherre the gyldedd bauble thatte envyronnes
" the heade of majeſtye noe norre honourres moſt
" weyghtye would give mee halfe the joye as didde
" thys mye lyttle worke forre thee The feelinge
" that dydde neareſte approache untoe itte was
" thatte whiche commethe nygheſte untoe God
" meeke ande gentle charytye forre thatte virtue

K 2   " O !

" O ! Anna doe I love doe I cheryfhe thee inne
" mye hearte forre thou art ass a talle cedarre,
" ftretchynge forthe its branches and fuccourynge
" the fmallere plants frome nyppynge winneterre
" orr the boyfteroufe windes Farewelle toe
" morrowe bye tymes I will fee thee tille thenne
" Adewe fweete Love.

" Thyne everre.

" Wm. Shakfpeare."

" Anna Hatherrewaye."

Upon the internal ftyle of the letter, as it is
natural to expect, the critic makes no obfervation.
Of the folid fenfe, with which it abounds, the
marks of a pregnant intellect which it difplays,
and the beauty of its diction, and imagery, he
takes no cognizance. He is ftill *apud minima.*
With a tafte fimilar to his, who in examining the
beauties of an ancient temple, fhould infpect the
ftones of which it was built, and analyze the mortar
which cemented them together, he attempts to
pick out a flaw in the orthography, and fuperfcription. Or, to ufe a more ludicrous comparifon as Prior has it of a twelfth-cake

He is but an *idle dreamer,*
Who leaves the pye, to gnaw the ftreamer.

As a fpecimen of this " obfcure diligence,"
I would

I would juft point out the frivolous exception to the letter, on the fcore of its omitting in the fuperfcription the ufual prepofitions *For* and *To.* I leave this exception without commenting upon it. Then we are told, by way of farther objection, that the lady was chriftened plain Anne not *Anna*; and that her name was not Hatherwaye but *Hathaway.*

I have not examined parifh regifters, nor looked into mouldy records, to afcertain the precife manner, in which fhe was chriftened. But this does not interfere with the argument, for names are not always pronounced with the pronunciation which was ufed at the chriftening. Befides there are innumerable inftances, in which vernacular names are pronounced with a Roman termination. But this advocate for the fame of the immortal bard, according to the character he has arrogated to himfelf, might have recollected that names were frequently written in this mode by Shakfpeare himfelf, in feveral of his dramas. Let him look to his Taming the Shrew.

" Thou art to me as fecret and as dear,
" As ANNA to the Queen of Carthage was."

Act. 2. Sc. 4.

Have we not alfo *Ifabella*, for Ifabel? *Mariana*

riana for Marianne, in Meafure for Meafure?
Katharina in the Taming of the Shrew. *Maria*
in Love's Labour Loft. Ditto, Twelfth Night.
For *Anna* Queen of Great Britain, fee Taylor the
Water Poet, f. ed. p. 250. *Anna Maria* Eftouteville,
and *Henrietta Maria*, daughter of Thomas Savage,
Vifcount Rock Savage, both born the end of the
16th, or the beginning of the 17th century.
Thefe inftances I am furnifhed with by F. Town-
fend, Efq. Windfor Herald.

Again we find in the Parifh Regifter of St.
Botolph Bifhopfgate, " Anna ——— one of the
" nunnies maides of St. Mary Spital, buried 20th
" of October, 1613. Thefe inftances, will I
think, fhew to conviction the frequent ufe of thefe
names, of *Anna* in particular, of which Mr. Malone has dogmatically faid that *in plain profe*, no
example can be produced in the fixteenth century.
Yet furely the letter to Anne Hatherwaye is not
plain profe. If that can only be called poetry,
which is expreffed in certain metre, and cadence,
this is certainly profe, and probably this gentleman
has no other criterion to diftinguifh between poetry, and profe. But if by poetry, be meant that,
which breathes infpiration, and is clothed in a fort
of numerous diction though not regular verfifica-
tion, then the letter I am fpeaking of, is furely
a poetical compofition.

With

With regard to the exceptionable fpelling of
Hatherrewaye, I fhall not trefpafs much on the
attention of the reader, by entering into minute
difquifition concerning it. This only I will remark, as far as the remark can apply to the fubject of the MSS, that Ben Jonfon's name is frequently written in papers which I have in my poffeffion, Johnfonne, and even the name of Har-
court, whofe name is fo fpelled in a printed book,
intitled, a Voyage to Guiana, has in a note immediately under it, in the very hand-writing of
the Shakfpeare MSS, the word fpelt *Harrecourte*.
Now, not to lay any emphafis on the queftion
of the authenticity or impofture of the papers, is
not this unufual mode of orthography as recon-
cileable to the one as to the other hypothefis ? for,
what forger in his fenfes would have betrayed fo
grofs an improvidence, as to difplay errors, which
muft have directly militated againft his own pur-
pofes. And though our critic is fo very confident, that the erroneous orthography of this
name, is a fufficient proof of the impofture, it is
no ftronger proof to a candid mind than the fpelling
of Lowine, Leycefterre, or Shakfpeare in feveral
oppofite and contradictory ways.

But, fays Mr. Malone, had the addrefs been
" my *fweet* Anne," inftead of *deareft*, it might have
paffed well enough. In fupport of this frivolous
remark,

remark, he cites Sir John Harrington, who begins his letter to his lady, dated December 27, 1602, with the words " Sweet Mall." In reply to this, I shall refer Mr. Malone to Lodge's Illustrations, where he will find in vol. 2. p. 102, in the Earl of Derby's letter, the words " Dearest Friend," used in 1589 : again in the same volume p. 72, we shall find " Dearest Py." In Nicol's Elizabeth's Progress, p. 7, in Churchyard's Pleasaunt Comedie, " My Deere, adiew.

But to quit the subject, we will refer this critic to his own quotations, particularly in p. 56, where Sir Philip Sidney addresses his Sister, " *To my deare* Lady and Sister the Countesse of " Pembroke." But it is of all labours, the most wearisome, and certainly the least instructive, to occupy our understandings about such miserable trash. In a note, it is observed by the critic, that the forgery is proved by the fact, namely, of misnomers, orthographies, &c. notwithstanding the reasons that might be adduced in support of them.

Admirable reasoning ! But how my good critic, is this fact proved ? Is it by my Lady Barnard's Will, or by the old Parish Register, which contains the marriage of a person, who is not even known to belong to that family ? Let us leave him, however, to his registers and prerogative indexes.

Now

Now with regard to the orthography of the poet's name (once more to recur to this topic) can any rational man conclude, that Heminge and Condell, the editors and printers of Shakfpeare's works, were forgers, becaufe they fpelt his name *Shakefpeare?* though in the only admitted autographs of the bard, he himfelf wrote it Shakfpere and Shakfpeare. And by the fame reafon in the inftance before us, namely, the fpelling of Hatherwaye, can the orthography of her name, not as it was written in her own hand, but as it was found in the will of a defcendant, in the third degree of generation from her, be according to any found principles of logic, or evidence, confidered as a forgery?

But not content with digreffing from his fubject by invocations to Venus, and the Graces, we now find our critic introducing his political opinions into the controverfy before us. In truth, there feems fome little ingenuity in the mode of procedure, which he has adopted. He feems to have known, that if all the refearches he has expended on the fubject, the minute, and laboured criticifms he has purfued, for the purpofe of invalidating the MSS, fhould be but little attended to, and their effect on the queftion but flightly eftimated, to introduce his political tenets, and to fhew a feditious tendency in fome paffage of the MSS would

L   excite

excite a powerful, and efficient prejudice againft them. For this purpofe, he introduces himfelf as a zealous royalift; and has felected a paffage of the above letter, to which he imputes a feditious con-ftruction. The words which he marks out as a contemptuous allufion to royalty are thofe of " *gyl-* " *dedde bawbles.*" Let me, however, requeft the reader to perufe the paffage. None, but the moft fervile courtier, can furely take an exception to any phrafe of this kind. In calling the crown a gilded bawble, Shakfpeare only repeated, what he has frequently faid in his dramas. Who is there that will mark out for animadverfion every fenti-ment, which concerns the emptinefs of royalty, and that occurs not only in this poet, but which muft occur in the works of all, who have ftudied hu-man life, and drawn rational reflections from the perufal of it? Who for inftance, could make this objection to the fpeech of Richard II.

———————— Within the hollow crown
That rounds the mortal temples of a king,
Keeps death his court, and there the antic fits,
Scoffing his ftate, and grinning at his pomp, &c.
                                        Act. 3. Sc. 4.

Still purfuing his digreffion, Mr. Malone at-
                                                tempts

tempts to give an eulogium on the character of Queen Elizabeth. As he has provoked the subject, I truft, that a flight obfervation on the character of this princefs, will be allowed me in my turn. It is intimated by Mr. Malone, that time may have abated the fplendor of her name. Perhaps there is no better proof than this, that the fplendor of her character was temporary and adventitious, rather than durable and folid. The moft unequivocal teft, to which the general policy or perfonal character of a fovereign can be brought, is the eftimate of a fair, and unbiaffed pofterity ; becaufe it is an eftimate, into which no temporary prepoffeffions, no heats of party, or faction can poffibly enter. It is indeed fomewhat remarkable that the example of this princefs, whom every hiftorian has reprefented to have been more tenacious, of the royal prerogative, and more avaricious of arbitrary fway, than any of her predeceffors, fhould be held up as an object of fuch ardent veneration. I know not how to account for it, but by attributing it to the new fafhioned propenfity, not only to contemplate with complacency, but even with admiration, thofe periods of our hiftory, in which the liberties of the people were the moft over looked, or defpifed. Mr. Malone in his abhorrence of regicide, ought not to have forgot the cruel murder of the Scottifh Queen, in which a lawful

and

and aimiable fovereign was depofed by the artful, and jealous policy of the princefs, of whom he is fo violently enamoured. The reign of this queen, however, was profperous, in the wars fhe entered into, and the commerce of the country was confiderably extended at that period. This will account for the predilections to this princefs. So true is it that a combination of profperous circumftances, will throw a fort of magnificence over a government, the adminiftration of which is uniformly conducted on the moft arbitrary, and tyrannical principles. With regard to the " deteftable doc- " trines of modern republicans," which our critic feems fo thoroughly to apprehend, I fhall only ob- ferve that if the caufe of regular governments, has no better fupport, than the pen of an half informed and cloudy commentator, it ftands in a ftate deplorably precsrious, and diffoluble.

But to return to the verbal objections of the critic. On the ufe of the word " bawble," in the letter to Anna Hatherwaye, he obferves, that he has fome doubt, whether the word had obtained that fignification, fo early as the middle of the reign of Elizabeth. He doubts whether it was ufed at that time, though in the foregoing fentence, he allows that it bears the very fenfe affixed to it in feveral of our poet's plays. Why, however, the world is to be fatisfied with the doubts of this gentleman,

gentleman, I am at a lofs to difcover, and I am
equally perplexed to difcern upon what principles
his doubts, unaccompanied as they are even with
the fhadow of an argument, can operate againſt
my reaſonings. In p. 14. we have produced inſtances uffieient to fhew that the word *Bawble* was
in ufe in Elizabeth's time, and long before that
period, and was applied exactly in the fenfe, in
which it is ufed in the MSS. In Cymbeline, a
play the commentator fhould certainly have had
ſome knowledge of, we find

> " Richer than doing nothing, for a *bauble*,
> " Prouder than rustling in unpaid for filk."

Another inſtance I fhall here adduce, (though it
is fcarcely neceffary) to prove the word was in very
common ufe in 1633. In the index of words prefixed to Butler's Englifh Grammar printed in that
year, and which confiſts of only twelve leaves, we
find under letter B. To Babble, Garrio, a *Bawble*,
Nugamentum.

With regard to the objection, that *gilded* is an
unfuitable epithet to diadem, and that Shakſpeare
muſt have known that the diadem always confiſted
of real gold, I fhall make but one obfervation.
It is evident from the fenfe to which it is applied
in the letter before us, that the epithet, " *gilded*," was
ufed

uſed in a derogatory manner, in order to degrade the value of the object to which he alludes. It is a figure in rhetoric, which Quintillian and Tully call the *imminutio*; and had Mr. Malone read the works of either of theſe writers, he would not ſurely have tried a mere metaphorical diction, by the teſt of rigid truth, to which it is abſurd to bring either figurative, or rhetorical expreſſion.

In order to ſhew, however, that the prevalent opinions of our author's age, were inconſiſtent with the ſentiment in the letter to Anne Hatherwaye, we have many quotations from Shakſpeare. But how looſe unconnected extracts from various plays, can demonſtrate the real ſentiments of the author, I cannot diſcover. When Shakſpeare wrote his dramas, he would naturally put into the mouths of his theatrical perſonages, the ſentiments which were the moſt congenial to their reſpective characters. He knew, that unleſs he was governed by this principle, the unity of character and action, which is the moſt prominent merit of Shakſpeare, would be violated and deſtroyed. He attributed, therefore, to his dramatic agents, their appropriate expreſſions. When a biſhop ſpeaks, Shakſpeare provided him with the language of paſſive ſubmiſſion to the reigning authority which it is natural for a biſhop to utter. In the lips of his ſove-

reigns,

reigns, he has put the diction of a confcious, and dignified fuperiority ; in thofe of his courtiers, the maxims of pliant and accomodating fervility. Hence it is, that in the writings of Shakfpeare, it is eafy to felect paffages, in which the moft fervile, and fubmiffive principles are inculcated. But on the other hand, it is by no means difficult to find fentiments, which breathe the fpirit of a proud and dignified independence. Paffages of this kind may be found in Julius Cæfar, and in many other plays, where it was neceffary for the prefervation of that unity of character, which appears in all his dramas, that appropriate fentiments and expreffion fhould be ufed.

But we have alfo an objection to the ufe of the word " cedar," and to the phrafe " forre thou arte as " a talle cedarre ftretchynge forthe its branches and " fuccourynge fmaller plants fromme nypyngge " winterre, or the boyfteroufe windes. It is faid " that an umbrageous multitude of leaves, inftead " of fuccouring deftroys all vegetation under it." This is not true. Mr. Malone has proved himfelf not only ignorant of natural hiftory, but even incapable of the moft obvious reflection. Vegetation, every one knows, requires air ; this is evident from the propenfity, which naturalifts have obferved in all plants, and fhrubs, to bend towards the air, when they are fituated in places, which

which do not admit a general circulation and dif-
fufion of that fluid. But we are yet to learn, that
the fhelter of a tree is unfavourable to the growth
of fmaller fhrubs and plants. Ivy, Jeffamine, the
Rofe-tree, and Ever-greens, flourifh always in the
fhade. This would-be critic here finds fault with
what he cannot underftand. I muft firft remind
him of the maxim of the fchools, " Nullum
" fimile eft idem," or to tranflate it to him,
" That which refembles any thing, cannot be the
" fame." If he finds fault with the above
beautiful paffage, what will he fay to the following effort of a great mafter? " My love is
" as the cyprefs in the garden, like the horfe in
" the chariots of Theffaly." I muft now inform
this God of Letters, that, if a refemblance is exact
throughout, it is not any longer, poetically fpeaking
a fimile. Has he forgot the objection againft Ad-
difon's angel, or does he not know it? Perhaps he
may not. But to anfwer him incontrovertibly, at
leaft in his own way, I affert, that fome ever-
greens and other plants will thrive beneath the
fhady branches of trees; and that in moft counties
famous for the production of apples, in order to
fave ground, grain is fown in the orchards, which
does not feem to flourifh the lefs from being fo fituated: and, laft of all, he muft be requefted to
perufe the lines in queftion again, and he will find,
that

that in them the cedar is fuppofed only to defend the fmaller plants " fromme nyppynge winneterre, " or the boyfteroufe windes ;" and not to fuccour vegetation, as he mifunderftood them. It is rational to infer, that when they are protected from the cold blafts, and in fouthern climates from the intenfe rays of the fun, they would be more hkely to thrive in their young and tender ftate. That vegetation, however, does flourifh under this fpecies of covering, is evident from the immenfe quantity of underwood, or low fhrubs, which will be obferved in all woods and forefts, where there is a great deal of fhade, and protection afforded them by the larger trees. Leaving however, this fpecies of digreffion, let us now examine the verfes by Shakfpeare, to Anna Hatherwaye.

" Is there inne heavenne aught more rare
" Thanne thou fweete nymphe of Avon fayre,
" Is there onne earthe a manne more trewe,
" Thanne Willy Shakfpeare is to you.

" Though fyckle fortune prove unkynde
" Still dothe fhe leave herre wealthe behynde
" She neere the hearte canne forme anew
" Norre make thye Willy's love untrue.

" Though age withe withered hand doe ftryke,
" The forme mofte fayre the face mofte bryghte,
" Stille dothe fhe leave untouchedde and trewe
" Thy Willy's love ande friendfhippe too.

M   " Though

" Though deathe with neverre faylynge blowe
" Dothe Manne and babe alyke brynge lowe
" Yette doth he take naughte butte hys due
" Ande ftrikes notte Willy's hearte ftill trewe.

" Synce thenne norre forretune death norre age
" Canne faythfulle Willy's love affuage
" Then doe I live ande dye forre you
" Thy Willye fyncere ande moft trewe."

The firft verbal exception to thefe ftanzas, is
the ufe of " Heavenne" as a dyffillable. The
exception is founded on the authority of Spenfer.
" In his letter to Gabriel Harvey, April 1580"
" Heaven being ufed fhort as one fyllable, when it is
" in verfe ftretched with a diaftole, is like a lame
" dog that holdeth up one leg. In our poet's ge-
" nuine compofitions, we never find any fuch hob-
" bling metre," obferves the commentator on Shakfpeare. To what purpofe he has read this great
mafter will be feen, from the fpecimens I fhall adduce, to fhew that it is ufed indifcriminately as a
diffylable and monyfyllable in various paffages of
his plays.

The means, that *Heaven* yields muft be embraced,
And not neglected : elfe if *Heaven* would,
And we would not *Heavn's* offer, we refufe
The proffered means of fuccour, and redrefs.
King Richard II. Act 3. Sc. 2.

——————— Oh ! you are men of ſtones,
Had I your tongues, and eyes, I'd uſe them ſo,
That *Heaven*'s vault ſhould crack : ſhe's gone for ever.
Lear. Act. 5.

Now let the rain of *Heaven* wet this place,
To waſh away my woeful monuments.
Henry VI. Part 2. Act. 3.

By *Heaven* I had rather coin my heart,
And drop my blood for drachmas, than to wring
From the hard hands of peaſants, their vile traſh
By any indirection.
Julius Cæſar, Act. 4.

The Sun not yet thy ſighs from *Heaven* clears.
Romeo and Juliet, Act. 2. Sc. 3.

Why e'en in that was *Heaven* ordinant.
Hamlet, Act. 5.

He finds the joys of *Heaven* here on earth.
Merchant of Venice.

I cannot 'twixt the *Heaven*, and the Main
Deſcry a ſail.
Othello, Act. 2.

I have tow'rd *Heaven* breath'd a ſecret vow.
Othello, Act. 2.

M 2

By

By *Heaven* I will ne'er come in your bed,
Untill I fee the King.

    Merchant of Venice, Act. 5.

Study is like the *Heaven*'s glorious Sun.

    Love's Labour Loft, Act. 1

Thefe earthly Godfathers of *Heaven*'s lights.
    ibid.

Heaven would in little fhew
Therefore *Heaven*'s nature's charg'd.

    As You Like it. Act. 3. Sc.

Hymen from *Heaven* brought her.
    ibid.

Make *Heaven* drowfy with the Harmony.
    Love's Labour Loft.

And Beauty's creft becomes the *Heavens* well.
    ibid.

What peremptory eagle-fighted eye
Dares look upon the *Heaven* of her brow.
    Love's Labour Loft.

———————————— In vaine do men
The *Heavens* of their fortunes fault accufe.
    Spenfer.

        Looke

Looke when the *Heavens* are to juftice beat.
Ibid.

The funne that meafures *Heaven* all day long
At night doth bath his fteeds, th' ocean waves among.
Ibid.

At laft the golden Orientall gate
Of greateft *Heaven* gan to open fayre,
And Phœbus frefh as bridegroome to her mate,
Came dauncing forth, fhaking his dewie haire,
And hurles his gliftering beames through gloomie ayre.
Ibid.

———————— Now the golden Hefperus
Was mounted hie in toppe of *Heaven*'s fheene.
Ibid.

It was the time, when reft foft fliding downe
From *Heaven*'s height, into man's heavie eyes
Ibid.

————————— Her angel's face
As the great eye of *Heaven* fhined bright.
Ibid.

What fo the *Heavens* in this fecret doombe,
Ordained have, how can fraile flefhy wight
Forecaft, but it muft needs to iffue come.
Ibid.

Why have I quoted thefe inftances? I have
quoted

quoted them to fhew that this gentleman, who we ought to fuppofe, is too converfant with Shak-fpeare, not to have met with thefe paffages, has made an affertion, which every page almoft of this author falfifies and deftroys. It were to be wifhed that this critic and hiftorian of *Lowine*, could be made to know fomething about what he writes, before he begins fcribbling, he would then con-trive to get fome underftanding of the author of whom he fpeaks. He would then know that Spenfer has taken this licence in as large a latitude as any of his neighbours,

> " Like as a tender rofe in open plaine
> " Difpreds the glory of her *leaves* gaye."

This is dilatation, this is diaftole with a ven-geance. But what reliance in any refpect, is to be had in the genius of vocabulary and dictionary ? old and new, from Romeus and Juliet to Samuel Johnfon, he has written and read " a world of " wordes;" but what does he know in any refpect of the ufe of them ? that he knows nothing of the meafure of either Shakfpeare or Spenfer, is here demonftrated, and yet he dreams that he is as familiar with them as his glove, and, as if they were fworn companions. We have feen that thofe who are utterly incapable of reafoning, can very glibly

glibly enumerate and run over the names of our old logicians; and Cockeran or Coles may help him to the meaning of the words, fyſtole and diaſtole, whom no ſchooling, no drudgery, no reading or tranſcribing, can make feel the harmony of numbers.

Not long after the critic's publication of his enquiry, we find him recanting his aſſertion, and proclaiming his ignorance through the medium of the Gentleman's Magazine, acknowledging that he recollects the uſe of the word in Macbeth.

> " Hear it not Duncan, for it is a knell,
> " That ſummons thee to *Heaven*, or to Hell.

And does this retractation atone for the temerity of making bold, and unſupported blunders, on a ſubject to which one might imagine from his peculiar ſtudy and avocation, he would have paid a ſtricter and more diligent attention. It appears rather extraordinary, that a commentator on Shakſpeare, ſhould convict himſelf of having never read him.

The next paper in the order purſued by Mr. Malone, is the

Letter from Shakſpeare to the
Earl of Southampton;
and the
Earl's anſwer.

Here

Here we come once more to affertions, urged if poffible with encreafed arrogance, and more deftitute than ever of proof, or reafon. It is faid, that there is not a fingle circumftance belonging to thefe letters, that does not detect and expofe the impofture. But the reader will fmile, when he obferves the extraordinary mode, in which this affeveration is attempted to be maintained. The reafoning is not fpecifically applicable to the letters before us, but comprehends the whole of the fubject. It does not merely attach fufpicion to this part of the Shakfpeare documents, but overwhelms in one indifcriminate torrent of refutation, the intire collection of manufcripts altogether. What is this irrefiftable argument? Stripping it of its ufelefs incumbrance of words, and bringing it into a narrow compafs, it is precifely this. *I, Edmund Malone, having been employed on a life of Shakfpeare for two years paft, and with the aid of authentic and indifputable documents, (which the world has not yet feen) having overturned every traditional ftory, concerning Shakfpeare for near a century paft (which is yet to be proved) not being unconverfant with the fubject, do pronounce thefe MSS to be fpurious.*

Mr. Malone is pleafed to confider thefe letters as formed on fome archetype, or received tradition concerning Shakfpeare. The letters in

quettion,

queftion, he afcribes to a tradition, tranfmitted from Sir William Davenant to Mr. Rowe, that Lord Southampton gave our author no lefs a fum than one thoufand pounds. But how is this act of patronage and liberality difproved ? Why Mr. Malone is poffeffed of indifputable documents, which prove what ? that this liberality muft have been greatly magnified, and that the ftory in all its parts cannot be true. Now let me requeft the reader to obferve, in the firft place that thefe *indifputable documents* are not produced ; that according to equitable rules of reafoning, therefore they have no weight at all in the prefent argument. In the fecond place, giving the critic credit for his *indifputable documents*, and allowing that they prove the liberality of Southampton to have been exaggerated in this tradition, as far as the queftion relates to the letters before us, they prove nothing at all, becaufe thefe letters fpecify no fum, but allude merely to an indefinite, though great act of bounty from the Earl to his friend Shakfpeare. But it is diverting to hear the critic prefcribe, in what order the correfpondence would have been conducted, had the poet received the mark of munificence from his noble patron, Firft, fays he, Lord Southampton's letter would fpecify the fum, which he had given, as a tribute to the talents of the great bard, and then we fhould have feen the

N   poet's

poet's letter of thanks. On what grounds, does Mr. Malone affert that fuch would have been the natural order of correfpondence ? Muft it have neceffarily happened, that this bounty was communicated by a letter, or if it was communicated by letter, might not this letter have been loft? But the inference which the commentator draws from the letters appearing in this order, is, that a fpecific fum muft have been mentioned, and that the fabricator was well aware, " *that fome inqui-* " *fitive refearcher like myfelf,*" would be poffeffed of documents, which would immediately afcertain the bounty to have been very different from the fum fixed upon. Here we are again naufeated with thofe eternal references to his documents, with which Mr. Malone has tormented his readers, almoft in every page of his work. In anfwer however to thefe objections, let me afk, whether it is abfolutely inconfiftent with the laws of human probability, that a nobleman of diftinguifhed rank, and more diftinguifhed for his patronage of ingenious and deferving men, fhould beftow on an author, like Shakfpeare, a great, and fignal munificence ? And whether the bard, while all the emotions of gratitude were ftruggling in his breaft, might not exprefs his feelings in the letter, which for the fecond time I here prefent to the public, together with the earl's reply.

Copye

Copye of mye letter toe hys grace offe Southampton.

Mye Lorde

Doe notte efteeme me a fluggarde nor tardye
for thus havynge delayed to anfwerre or rather toe
thank you for youre greate bountye I doe affure
you my gracioufe and good lorde that thryce I have
effayed toe wryte and thryche mye efforts have
beene fruitleffe I know notte what toe faye Profe
Verfe alle all is naughte gratitude is all I have toe
utter and that is tooe great and tooe *fublyme a feeling* for poore mortalls toe exprefs O my lord itte
is a budde which blloffommes blloms but never
dyes itte cherifhes fweete nature and lulls the calme
Breaft to fofte fofte repofe Butte mye goode lorde
forgive thys mye departure fromme mye fubjecte
which was toe returne thankes and thankes I doe
returne O excufe mee mye lord more at prefentte
I cannotte

> Yours devotedlye and with due refpecte
> Wm. Shakfpeare

Lord Southampton's anfwer.

Deare Willam

I cannotte doe leffe than thanke you forre
youre kynde letterre butte whye deareft Freynd

talke

talke fo much offe gratitude mye offerre was double the fomme butte you woulde accept butte the halfe therefore you neede notte fpeake foe muche on thatte fubjeฬte as I have beene thye freynde foe I will continue aughte that I can doe forre thee pray commande mee and you fhall fynde me

Yours Southampton.

[Superfcribed]
" To the Globe Theatre
" For Mafter William
" Shakfpeare."

To the *orthography*, the objeฬion of Mr. Malone is the fame, as that which I confidered in the former part of this work. As to the addrefs of " Your Grace" the reafonings I have urged, on its ufe in the other letters, will apply with the fame force to that, which is now under our confideration.

Inftead of " *Mye Lorde*" with which the letter commences, it fhould have been Right Honorable I fhall not enter at large into this objeฬion, becaufe this gentleman in the fubfequent fentence has faved me the trouble of adverting to it, by acknowledging that " *Right Honorable*" was not the only mode of that time, the other being fometimes ufed. What credit is due to a writer, who in the

very

very fame fentence hazards the moft unqualified affertions, and the completeft retractations to annul, and falfify them ?

The part of the letter, which next falls under our critic's animadverfion, are the following words " *thryce* I have effayed toe write, and *thryce* mye " efforts have been fruitleffe." Thefe, he fays, are borrowed from Ovid.

" Ter conata loqui, ter fletibus ora rigavit." But in a ftyle of farcaftic contempt, he obferves, that he entirely acquits the author of ever having read Ovid, and that he was indebted to Milton's imitation of his favorite poet.

" Thrice he effayed, and thrice, in fpight of fcorn, " Tears fuch as Angels weep burft forth."

There is perhaps no office in criticifm, which is more truly contemptible, than that to which Mr. Malone, and other commentators have afpired; I mean, that of tracing the diction of one author into that of another. They are a fort of Bow-ftreet runners in literature. They are employed in fearching for ftolen goods, where ever their fagacity, which is not of the higheft kind, may direct them. No fubject of criticifm therefore has been more abufed, and none has been undertaken by weaker, or more taftelefs illuftrators. I do not

deny,

deny, that the comparifon of parallel beauties, and the difplay of ftriking refemblances in different writers may contribute to good tafte and to literature ; nor can I deny, that this tafk has been executed by deep, and accomplifhed critics. But thefe great men have often allowed too liberal a fcope for their own fancies and caprices on thefe topics ; fo that others, of no critical pretenfion, and no critical fagacity, have been feduced by their ex-ample, and have exerted their unprofitable diligence, in following the fuggeftions of their own underftandings, which no ray of genius, or tafte ever condefcended to vifit.

Hence it is, that thefe gentlemen have been fo often flattered with the notion of having made a wonderful difcovery, if they ftumble on a fingle word, or a fingle phrafe, which through the twilight of a confufed memory, they think they have feen in other authors. One of Shakfpeare's commentators (I forget whether it was Mr. Malone) when the great bard puts into the mouth of one of his characters " Go before I'll follow, finds it out to be an allufion to a paffage in Terence" I præ te fequar. And Dean Swift fomewhere adverts to one of thefe fagacious critics, who in order to prove that he was indebted for his Tale of the Tub, to a French book entitled Combat des Livres, cites the phrafes " *If I mifremember not,*" and " *I am*
" *affured,'*

' *affured*," which he fays, he found in the French author. Thefe taftelefs commentators are the very plague and bane of literature; and are a fort of poifonous weeds that grow up in the fweeteft flowers of Parnaffus; as Lucretius expreffes it on another occafion,

Eft etiam in magnis Heleconis montibus arbor
Floris odore hominem tetro confueta necare.

But to return to the phrafe before us. Is there any reafon to fuppofe, that Milton found the archetype of his own expreffion in Ovid; or that Shakfpeare in this, (or his forger), fhould have copied from Milton? Is not the repetition of the word " thrice," a common figure in rhetoric? Did Dryden copy from either of thefe poets, when he exclaims in his ode to St. Cecilia,

" And thrice he routed all his foes,
" And thrice he flew the flain."

This is furely a fpecies of criticifm, which is founded on principles, fo vague, and indefinite, that no rational man would ever propofe it, as a teft, to which a controverfy of the prefent nature fhould be brought. It is, however, curious to attend to the perfonal farcafms of the critic, when he fays that he " *perfectly acquits the author of* " *having*

" *having read Ovid.*" Had Mr. Malone been able to read Homer, he would have found this mode of expreſſion was his originally, but of this " *I entirely acquit him.*"

Whether Mr. Malone is intimately acquainted with the ſuppoſed forger of theſe papers or not, the ſarcaſm is lame and impotent, to whatever quarter it might have been directed. Whether the perſon, alluded to, has read Ovid or not, if any ſuch perſon exiſts, which Mr. Malone has not proved, it would be impoſſible to aſcertain. But for my own part, I ſhould prefer as a critic, and a ſcholar, the man, who never peruſed a ſingle line of Ovid, to him, who after all his reading, has neither ſenſibility to feel, nor capacity to underſtand that which he has read. I ſhould prefer the man, who neither disfigures, nor defaces the literature, which lies within his reach, to him, whoſe knowledge is only acquired by rummaging the indexes, ſettling the punctuations, or exploring the dates of the writings that ſurround him.

Mr. Malone then finds another paſſage in this obnoxious letter, viz. when the poet tells his patron that " gratitude is a budde which blloſſomes, " bllooms, butte never dyes ; itte cheriſhes " ſweete nature, ande lulls the calme breaſte toe " ſofte, ſofte repoſe." Not to employ ourſelves any further with the orthography, on which ſo

much

much has been faid already, the good fenfe of the paffage is, I think but flightly affected by the critic's objection. He infinuates that Shakfpeare was too good a naturalift not to know, that a bud firft blooms, and then bloffoms. And fo it may be in Ireland, but in England, we are accuftomed to fay, that a tree firft bloffoms, but continues in bloom. Admitting the critic to be right, it is juftified by the figures, Hyfteron and Proteron.

" There I was bred and born."

Then we have a piece of elaborate hyper-criticifm, to prove that Dr. Warburton ufed the words " lulls our overwearied nature to repofe," in one of his notes on Shakfpeare, and that this paffage in the letter was plagiarized from it. Here, however, I fhall leave Mr. Malone to his own triumph, and fhall only obferve, that it is a coincidence which might eafily be accounted for, by thofe, who have the flighteft obfervation, or good fenfe. The fame emotions will generally fpeaking, dictate nearly the fame language. Shakfpeare in defcribing the foothing effect of gratitude in the breaft that cherifhes it, could not find a combination of words more fuited to him, than thofe at which our commentator is difpofed to cavil: and Dr. War-

O   burton,

burton, when he fought to convey an idea of that,
which frees and difengages the mind from care,
would as naturally exprefs himfelf in the fame diction. If Mr. Malone's be found criticifm, the
greater part of human compofition is a plagiarifm
it being impoffible to avoid cafual coincidencies or
even ftriking refemblances, where there exifts an
uniformity of circumftances, and an identity of
feeling in the different writers.

Mr. Malone next obferves, that the conclufion
of the letter is completely modern ; " Oh, excufe
" me, mye lorde, more at prefente I cannorte."

" Yours devotedlye and with due refpecte"

He objects to " *at prefente*" and to " *with due*
" *refpecte*," which he fays are equally modern, as
well as objectionable. Mr. Malone on this topic,
obferves, that there is a fafhion, in the ftyle, and
conclufion of letters. I agree with him, to the
full extent of his obfervation. But does it follow,
that this fafhion prefcribes precifely the fame terms
and the fame phrafes ? Certainly not. The forms
which at this time, prevail in letter-writing, either
in the addrefs, or the conclufion, vary widely from
each other. One man, fays, " your humble fer-
" vant: another your devoted and obliged humble
" fervant," through an infinite variety of modifications. Now is it not very unfair reafoning, in referring to the forms of the times, on which we are now
occupied,

occupied, to set down any deviation from a specific form, which might have prevailed at that period, as a forged, and unauthentic document? But, says Mr. Malone, the letter will not pass for the composition of our poet, till an example be produced of a person in so low a situation, as that of a *player*, presuming to conclude a letter to a nobleman with the modern familiar assurance of attachment, " Yours most " devotedly." In reply to this, let me ask, whether Shakspeare, at the time, he is supposed to have written this letter, stood in the mere rank and estimation of a " *poor player* ?" Does not the critic know, that he was a poet, as well as actor; and that in every age, and period, the man of genuis, has been exalted almost to an equality with the patrons, that have encouraged and assisted him? I contend therefore, that without any impropriety, and consistently with the relations that subsisted between him, and Southampton, Shakspeare might make use of the form, in which he subscribed his letter to that nobleman.

Now for the answer of the Earl to this epistle. The first verbal objection to the letter is urged against the style of address " Deare William." Here as usual, Mr. Malone dictates what was the precise mode of beginning a letter, at the time of which we are speaking. With regard to its being imcompatible with the immeasurable distance, at

which

which Shakfpeare ftood from Lord Southampton, I affirm again, that there is nothing in the familiarity of addrefs at all irreconcileable to the fpecies of connection, between our bard and his noble patron. The great have in all times lived in habits of familiarity with enlightened and ingenious men, and this is not the only inftance, in which this familiarity is obfervable. But why fhould I repeat an obfervation, which I have been compelled fo frequently to make, concerning the temerity of laying down any precife or determinate form of expreffion, as the only mode, which prevailed at a fpecific period of time. Is it poffible for Mr. Malone, or any other antiquary, to have examined a thoufandth part of the letters, written at that time ? Why therefore, fhould he draw fuch particular and minute conclufions, from fuch general and indefinite premifes. Mr. Malone, knows as well as any body, that though there are general charaderiftical forms of expreffion, that belong to every age, that there will always be minute exceptions and deviations from habits, however fettled, and eftablifhed. Befides, we are loft in a world of uncertainty on this fubjed, when we attempt to frame a pofitive, and dogmatical opinion upon it. And perhaps, fo little do we know concerning it, that the very fpecimens, which Mr. Malone adduces to decide on the prevailing pradice of the time

may

may only be in fact, deviations, and exceptions from the general rule, of which the records and monuments, may have been deftroyed by time, and accident.

In page 107, I remarked upon the familiar terms of addrefs ufed at the period we are now fpeaking of, and amongft the reft, I inftanced " Dearefte friende" 1589; " Dearefte Py ;" and again " My Deere Adiew." In the concluding fentence of the letter, the objeéor has the thread-bare animadverfion of its being too familiar, con-fidered as the language of a nobleman to a player. Need I again recall the reader of this work, to the peculiar fpecies of relation which fubfifted be-tween thefe eminent men. Why does Mr. Ma-lone, by applying to Shakfpeare the mere cha-raéter, and defignation of the player, overlook altogether his greater diftinétion of a poet ; and not of a poet only, but of one, whom every age does not fee, and to whom the world is naturally, and irrefiftibly difpofed to pay a fort of homage, that is allied to idolatry. If, however, after what has been faid upon this fubjeét, it is at all necef-fary, to quote authorities in fupport of the epif-tolary ufages, which we have been difcuffing, I will refer to Burleigh's State Papers, where it appears that the mode of ending letters, was capricious, and variable. " Your affured loving friend" in a

letter

letter to Sir William Cecil; " Yours always af-
" fured, Secretary Petre to Secretary Cecil."
Your own affuredly, from the fame perfon, and an
infinite number of modifications, all which differ
confiderably from each other.

Next follows a minute examination, refpecting
the fignature Southampton. I will quote the critic's
own words. In the reign of Elizabeth," fays he,
" as your lordfhip knows, noblemen in their fig-
" natures, ufually prefixed their chriftian name to
" their titles ; as their ladies, and my lords, the
" bifhops, do at this day." But it is worth
while attending to the refervations in which
Mr. Malone whenever he finds his general pofition
untenable, endeavours to fhelter himfelf. He fays
this was the ordinary practice, though a few peers
deviated from that mode, and fubfcribed their titles only. So completely miftaken, however, in
his general propofition is the fagacious commentator, that he will find a double proportion of inftances againft him, if he had taken the trouble
of making refearches into the fubject. I refer to
the Shrewfbury MSS in the College of Arms,
where there will be found with innumerable others,
the following inftances againft the remark of Mr.
Malone.

Nottingham

Nottingham	Suffolk
Howard	Devonshire
Stafford	Northumberland
Lumley	Lisle
Pembroke	Salisbury
Cranbourne	Fenelon.

If it is neſſary to refer to an earlier period, ſee Burleigh's State Papers, p. 442, &c. &c. where it will be obſerved, that there are ſeven examples of the Duke of Norfolk's letters having the ſignature of Norfolk. In the ſame work, p. 507, and 520, Lord Boyd, ſigns only Boyd. In page 537 and 552, there is the ſimple ſignature of "Lumley." In 568 Pembroke, and 569 Arundell. I ſhall bring forward no other documents on a ſubjeĉt, which a very few authorities will illuſtrate, it would be only an unprofitable but laborious idleneſs to expatiate. As to the aſſertion that Lord Southampton uniformly ſigned H. Southampton, it is obſervable, that it is ſupported by no other proof than the two ſpecimens from the Harleian Colleĉtion, and no argument therefore can be adduced to prove that he never wrote his name in any other mode. *De apparentibus & non existentibus eadem est ratio.* I obſerve alſo, that in the eyes of the moſt eminent antiquaries, theſe papers bear little or no reſemblance to the hand-writing of the age.

Let

Let me urge the reader to examine how far my
affertion is grounded on fact, by an infpection of
the fpecimens, publifhed by Mr. Malone. The
reader who cafts his eye over the two fpecimens of
this nobleman's hand-writing in the plate, which
this gentleman has publifhed, will obferve as wide
a diffimilarity in the fize and form of the letters,
and in the fignature efpecially, as would be obferved, in the hand-writing of two diftinct individuals. Now where there are two autographs only,
and in each of thefe the fignatures differ, how can
any man endued with common fenfe, poffitively
affirm either of them fpecifically to be the ordinary mode, in which the nobleman alluded to,
wrote his name? To fum up his objections to the
letter, the critic is pleafed to call the whole " falfe
" and hollow" a miferable, bungling, nonfenfical
forgery. Has Mr. Malone, entered into any reafonings upon the internal merits of thefe letters?
If he has not, (as the reader has had ample opportunity of remarking) difcuffed them, and duly confidered their ftyle and beauty, but has picked out the
little exceptions againft them, on the fcore of orthography, and epiftolary ufage, this choice and ele-
gant combination of epithets is contemptible, and
ridiculous.

The profeffion of faith next prefents itfelf, as a
fubject for Mr. Malone's animadverfion. Paffing

over

over the date, and orthography, the firſt topic, on which our critic enlarges, is grounded on the aſſumption of its being derived, in the ſame manner as ſome other of the documents, from ſome ſuppoſed model or archetype. It was formed, ſays he, " on a confeſſion of faith written by one John " Shakſpeare, which I (Mr. Malone) publiſhed " in the end of the year 1790." This paper however from ſubſequent circumſtances turns out not to be genuine; ſo that for the ſecond time the gentleman himſelf acknowledges that his own blunders and confuſion reſpecting a document, he imagined to be authentic, have proved the ſource of future forgeries of a ſimilar kind. From the confeſſions, however, which the critic is accuſtomed to make, from time to time, upon this ſubject, it ſhould ſeem, that he has much to anſwer for, at the public tribunal, for the confident publication of impoſtures, which at one time, he is pleaſed to obtrude on the world, and at another ſhameleſsly to retract, and diſavow.

But I ſhall take the liberty of exhibiting to the world, what the ſagacious gentleman, ſtyles a myſtical rhapſody.

P

PRO-

PROFESSION OF FAITH.

I beynge nowe offe founde Mynde doe hope
thatte thys mye wyfhe wille atte my deathe bee ac-
ceeded too as I nowe lyve in Londonne ande as
mye foule maye perchance foone quitte thys poore
Bodye it is mye defire thatte inne fuch cafe I maye
bee carryed to mye Native place ande thatte mye
Bodye bee there quietlye interred wythe as little
pompe as canne bee ande I doe nowe inne theefe
mye feyrioufe Moments make thys mye profeffione
of fayth and whiche I doe moft folemnlye believe
I doe fyrfte looke toe oune lovynge and greate
God ande toe hys glorioufe fonne Jefus I doe alfo
beleyve thatte thys mye weake and frayle Bodye
wille retturne toe dufte but forre mye foul lette
God judge thatte as toe hymfelfe fhalle feeme
meete O omnipotente ande greate God I am fulle
offe Synne I doe notte thynke myfelfe worthye offe
thye grace ande Yette wille I hope forre evene
the poore pryfonerre whenne bounde with gallyng
Irons evenne hee wille hope for Pittye and whenne
the teares offe fweet repentance bathe hys wretched
pillowe he then looks and hopes forre pardonne

thenne

thenne rouze mye Soule and lette hope thatte
sweete cherisher offe alle afforde thee comforte alsoe
O Manne whatte arte thou whye considereste thou
thyselfe thus grately where are thy great thye boast-
ed attrybutes buryed loste forre everre inne colde
Deathe O Manne why attempteft thou toe searche
the greatnesse offe the Almightye thou doste butte
loose thye labourre more thou attemptéfte more
arte thou loste tille thye poore weake thoughtes
arre elevated toe theyre summite ande thence as
snowe fromme the leffee Tree droppe ande dif-
ftylle themselves tille theye are noe more O God
Manne as I am frayle bye Nature fulle offe Synne
yette greate God receyve me toe thye bofomme
where alle is sweete contente ande happynesse alle
is blysse where discontent isse neverre hearde butte
where oune Bonde offe freyndfhippe unytes alle
Menne Forgive O Lorde alle oure Synnes ande
withe thye grete Goodnesse take usse alle to thye
Breafte O cherishe usse like the sweete Chickenne
thatte under the Coverte offe herre spreadynge wings
Receyves herre lyttle Broode and hoeverynge
oerre themme keepes themme harmlesse ande in
safetye.

W^m. SHAKSPEARE.

With refpect to the incidental obfervation of the orthography, and phrafeology, to which he brings the fame thread-bare and fenfelefs exceptions, I refer to what I have fo amply obferved in a former part of this work. But the internal characteriftics of it, the fimple effufions of a fincere piety which it breathes, and the folemn and dignified diction it every where difplays, are not, I truft, affected by the taftelefs abufe of fuch a critic as Mr. Malone. There are however fome minute particularities of phrafeology, on which as he has beftowed a confiderable portion of obfervation, it behoves me by no means to difregard.

The firft paffage felected for remark, is the allufion to the *Chicken*, that fpreads her wings for the protection of her brood. That it fhould have been fuggefted by the paffage in the New Teftament, will not operate as a deduction from its beauty as a compofition, or from the proof in favor of its authenticity. As to the inapplicability of the word " *chicken*," on which fome ftrefs is laid, I fhall not detain my readers with minute, and frivolous remarks on the diftinction between a hen, and a chicken. Without, however, taking up the fubject as a matter of Natural Hiftory, it muft be obvious to all, that the word Chicken is a general term for the male and female fpecies of this fowl; and in this fenfe, none but the moft

deter-

determined, and incorrigible caviller can find any fault with the correctneſs of the expreſſion. Before however I quit this part of our ſubject, I would proteſt againſt a propoſition, laid down by Mr. Malone, with his characteriſtic confidence, that theſe apparent departures from veriſimilitude, on which he has alluded are obvious artifices, to give an air of authenticity to the whole, on the principle that a forger would have carefully avoided them. Now, I would aſk, whether this mode of procedure has been followed by forgers in general ? Have they not, in all the inſtances, we have at preſent on record, diligently endeavoured, to throw the veil of truth, and probability over their productions. Mr. Malone might with equal reaſon, contend that he who forged a bank-note, and avoided all reſemblance or analogy to his archetype would be as ingenious and ſucceſsful as if he had imitated the aſpect and characteriſtics of that, which he wiſhed to repreſent.

We now come to another verbal topic, I mean, the exception to the uſe of the word *accede*, as not being the phraſe of the age, in which Shakſpeare flouriſhed. Here is an opportunity of triumph to the critic. A word, which bears not a general and acknowledged acceptation in the time, to which it is aſcribed, he immediately ſeizes as his natural prey. At what period, the word *accede*

cede in its prefent interpretation, firft glided into ufe, it is impoffible to afcertain, nor has the objector himfelf attempted to prove. I will not turn to the lexicons, and gloffaries of the age. Thefe are not authorities, for the ufe of words, which are always implicitly to be followed. Moft unqueftionably in thofe days, as in the prefent, terms were ufed, which the compilers of dictionaries either overlooked or refufed to recognize. How many words at this time may be found in the correcteft writers, which it would be in vain to hunt for in any dictionary, or gloffary exifting, words however, which though they are deftitute of authority or precedent, are ftill juftified by the analogy, and principles of the language. Befides who has coined new words with greater licence than Shakfpeare ? But I will not reft on the probability, that the verb accede was in ufe at this time ; becaufe the fecondary and derivative word (accefs) had obtained the fame conftruction. I will do more, I will fhew from the authority of Florio's, dictionary publifhed in 1611, that the word " accedere ;" to *accede*, to *affent unto*, was known, and conftantly in ufe at that time. Another proof of the ignorance of the commentator, as to the ufe of words in the time of Shakfpeare. I cannot take my leave of this topic, without befeeching the reader, to compare the

Profeffion

Profeffion of Faith, which I have publifhed, with that edited by Mr. Malone in the year 1790. The ridiculous cant, and jargon with which this detected impofture overflows, forms the moft ftriking contraft to the fublime and pious fimplicity, which conftitutes the prominent merit of the former compofition. In his critical animadverfions on the beauty of its ftyle, I am willing to be at iffue with fuch a writer as this gentleman; when I may fhelter myfelf under the refpectable authority (with many others) of the venerable Dr. Jo. Warton, who on perufing it, obferved with much energy, " *that* " *though there were many beauties in the liturgy of our* " *church, yet this compofition far furpaffed them all!*"

The next piece, on which Mr. Malone employs his critical powers, is the letter from Shakfpeare to Richard Cowley, *a low actor*, as he is called, that played the part of Verges in *Much Ado About Nothing*? That a perfon, who performed the character was neceffarily a low actor, is a very unfair infinuation. Would any man be bold enough to call Mr. Garrick a *low actor*, becaufe he played Scrub, or Abel Drugger? And where is the hiftory of Cowley to be found to juftify Mr. Malone in his affertion that Cowley was a *low actor*, except from the fuppofition of his playing in Much Ado About Nothing? His theatrical powers might indeed be limited, but it is very

probable

probable, that he might have held in private life, that fair and honorable eftimation, that might have entitied him to the honour of our poet's friendfhip. What the critic, however objects to more particularly in this paper, are the two words " *wittye* " *and whimficalle*" in the following paffage. Ha- " vinge alwaye accountedde thee a pleafaunte and " *wittye* perfonne and oune whofe companye I doe " much efteeme, I have fent thee inclofedde a " *whimficalle* conceyte."

To the word " *wittye*" it is objected, that in our author's time, it was ufed exclufively in the fenfe of cunning, fhrewdnefs, and applied to the intellectual powers in general. In anfwer to this, I refer the commentator of Shakfpeare, to Shakfpeare himfelf.

Val. " Sir Thurio borrows his wit from your
" ladyfhip's looks, and fpends what he
" borrows kindly in your company.
Two Gent. of Verona.
Act. 2, S. 4.

" That I had my good wit out of the
" Hundred merry tales."
Much Ado About Nothing.
Act. 2, S. 1.

In the fifth act of the fame play Claudio fays to Benedict, " we are high proof melancholy, and " would fain have it beaten away. Wilt thou ufe " thy *wit* ?

What does this mean, but a requeft, that Benedict would exert his powers of humour to difpel the melancholy, of which he complained ?

Again, in As You Like It, Act 5. Sc. 1.

William. " Ay, Sir, I have a pretty *wit*."

And in Second Part of Henry V. Sc. 4, Falftaff fays

" I am not only *witty* in myfelf, but the caufe that " *wit* is in other men."

Thefe quotations are fufficient to fhew, that the word was ufed at that time, in the peculiar fenfe, which Mr. Malone's objection denies it, as well as in the more general and enlarged interpretation.

Upon the word " *whymficalle*" we have references to the dictionaries of Cotgrave, Cole, and the other lexicographers of the critic. I fhall fpeak very little on this head. Dictionaries never admit words, which have not been in received and eftablifhed ufe. Now, I do not contend that the objected word had arrived at this general acceptation, before the time of Shakfpeare, or had obtained fuch a general currency, as to introduce it into the compilations of Mr. Malone's literary

Q   favorites,

favorites, Cole and Cotgrave. But every word muſt have had its birth, and firſt introduction into the language. Dr. Johnſon traced this word no higher than Addiſon. Addiſon would probably, have referred him to ſome ſource, whence he derived it, and that ſource would probably have led to another. So that if it is impoſſible to point out the preciſe period, of its primary introduction, the preſumptive argument is as much in my favor, as in that of Mr. Malone ; as it is equally as fair to aſcribe the firſt uſe of it to Shakſpeare, as to any other writer.

But it was an innovation by no means inconſiſtent with the principles of our language. All derivative languages like the Engliſh, are in a ſtate of perpetual progreſſion. Hence new words, at the mere diſcretion of a popular writer have been derived from the latin. Subſtantives and verbs require their ſeveral adjectives ; and every one, in the unſettled periods of our diction, thought himſelf endued with a licence to derive adjectives from nouns, in general uſe, controlled by no other rule, than the common analogies of the tongue. The word *whim*, a contraction probably of *whim-wham*, was uſed at that time in the ſenſe applied to *whimſical*. It has been before obſerved, that Shakſpeare availed himſelf of the privilege of coining new words ; and when ſo convenient a

phraſe,

phrafe, as the adjective of *whim*, held out a temptation, it is natural to fuppofe, that he did not refift it. We have indeed an inftance in which Shakfpeare has ufed the word *whimpled*, when fpeaking of Cupid.

" *This whimpled, whining, purblind, wayward boy.*"

Dr. Johnfon fuppofes it to come from *whimper*, which has the fame meaning, as *whine*. Now befides the abfurdity of charging this beautiful paffage with fo grofs a tautology, it is contrary to the principles of our language, to fuppofe that *whimper* in its participle will be *whimpled*. It is not natural to fuppofe that it is compounded of " *whim-led*," which fignifies " humorous, fantaf- " tical" &c ? So that, if this conjecture be probable, there can remain fcarcely a doubt concerning the general acceptation of the word, and it is no violent conjecture to fuppofe, that Shakfpeare might have given a common word the ufual termination of an adjective. I have now trefpaffed confiderably on the patience of the reader, in following Mr. Malone through the greater part of the intricate labyrinth of verbal objections, in which he has involved the fubject. But much remains to be faid upon the other documents, againft which our critic is pleafed to take exceptions. What next prefents itfelf to our confideration, is the

Q 2   DEED

DEED of GIFT
To William Henry Ireland.

Mr. Malone obferves farcaftically, that this is the firft deed he ever perufed, where a ftory was fo regularly and circumftantially told. Now it is worthy of remark, that the critic has prefented the deed in fo defective and mutilated a form, that it is impoffible to pronounce with precifion concerning it, from his ftatement of it. The beginning of the deed runs thus. " I William " Shakfpeare of Statford on Avon but now livyng " in London neare unntoe a yard calledd or knowne " bye the name of Irelands yarde in the Black- " fryars London nowe beyinge att thys preafaunte " tyme of found mynde" &c. &c. " I didde " with my own hande fyrfte wryte on Papere the " contents hereof butte for the moure feçurytye " ande thatte noe difpute whatever myghte hap- " penne after my death," &c. Here then is an anfwer to every objection, that may be grounded on the informality of the deed, namely, the confeffion made by Shakfpeare himfelf of his having written it in the manner, which his own mind fuggefted to him.

But the firft objection is an anachronifm, which it feems, Mr. Malone has found in the Inftrument. Shakfpeare

Shakfpeare in this deed, it is faid, defcribes himfelf as living at Blackfryars in October, 1604.
But it is manifeft, fays Mr. Malone, that the
King's fervants were not then poffeffed of the
Blackfryars. What does this prove, allowing the
objection in point of fact to be valid? Why it
does not falfify a fyllable of what appears on the
face of the deed. If the Theatre was not at
Blackfryars, might not the poet have refided in
that part of the metropolis? Nothing that con-
tradicts fuch a fuppofition, can be found in the
hiftory of his life.

Let us attend to the remark upon the circum-
cumftance recorded in the deed, of the accident
on the Thames. Whether Shakfpeare could fwim,
fays the fagacious gentleman, I have no means of
afcertaining. Now it is rather furprizing, that he
who could take the gage, and dimenfions of Elizabeth's hand-writing, and could afcertain with
fuch accuracy the progreffive fizes, to which it ex-
panded as fhe advanced in life, fhould not be able
to inform the world, whether Shakfpeare was an
adept in fwimming, and point out the place, where
he fwam, and the diftance to which his art would
enable him to fwim. I think it however extremely
probable, fays the critic from the admirable lines
in the Tempeft, that he was well acquainted with
that ufeful art. Can any remark be more truly
abfurd?

abfurd? Does it neceffarily foilow, that Shakfpeare was verfed in the myfteries of every art,
occupation, or myftery to which he has alluded in
his writings? It is a fact that the poet Thomfon
was perfectly unacquainted with the fcience of
fwimming, which he has defcribed with fuch glow-
ing eloquence, and with fuch minute accuracy.
It is then infinuated, as an incongruous and contradictory circumftance, that none of his friends,
nor the boatmen, but only W. H. Ireland fhould
have attempted his refcue. Does Mr. Malone
fuppofe that every boatman, who navigates a fmall
boat on the Thames is verfed in the art of fwimming? I am afraid were Mr. M. himfelf to de-
pend on fuch affiftance, were a fimilar accident to
befal him, that his fpecific gravity would very
foon reach the bottom of the river, efpecially if
he had a bundle of his notes on Shakfpeare in his
pocket. But as to the affected banter of ftripping
off his jerkyn, &c. Let me afk whether any one,
who had the fmalleft degree of firmnefs, at fuch a
moment, or the flighteft regard for the life of another, would make an attempt of this nature without throwing off the incumbrances of drefs as
quickly as he could, which at that time were very
heavy, and would neceffarily have obftructed the
the action of his limbs on fuch an occafion?

As to the word *upfet*, which Mr. Malone cen-
fures,

iures, as a word of modern growth, the only grounds on which it is objected to are, that it is not to be found in Johnson's Dictionary, and that he (Mr. M.) has not met with it. To these objections I answer that Dr. Johnson, it is well known, has omitted several hundred words in general acceptation. Mr. Herbert Croft goes so far as to say thousands. As to the objection, I should be ashamed seriously to refute the absurd position that the critic lays down, *that no word can be genuine, with which he himself is unacquainted.*

Passing over the useless disquisition, which Mr. Malone has protruded into his work, concerning the William Henry Ireland mentioned in the deed, we are once more arrived at verbal discussions. In a conveyance to Shakspeare (now in the possession of Mr. Wallis) the tenement which he purchased, says the critic, is described, as having been " some-
" tymes in the tenure of James Gardyner, Esquire,
" and since that in the tenure or occupation of one
" William Ireland, or of his assignees or assigns."
Now mark the ingenuous inference of the critic.
" From the prefix *one*, the want of the addition
" of *Gent.* and the word *occupation*, which at
" that time was a word, that denoted trade, I had
" no doubt that he was a tradesman." A piece of more contemptible criticism, than the acceptation, which is applied to the word occupation by

Mr.

Mr. Malone, never difgraced the pages of any man, who pretended to criticifm, or literature. The word *occupation* did at the period to which I am alluding, as well as at the prefent time, mean nothing more, than that the houfe was occupied by the perfon alluded to. As to the infertion of the double name of *William Henry* Ireland, on which the prefumption of fraud is grounded by Mr. Malone, I would obferve, that if, as Mr. Malone fuppofes, the forger had copied the authentic deed in which there was only a fingle chriftian name, he muft have been extremely inexpert, and blindly ftupid in the fabrication, had he not made his copy with a ftricter accuracy.

Then we are informed, that in the laft century and long after it, perfons of the firft rank in England contented themfelves with one chriftian name. It feems that our laborious inveftigator has looked into lifts of the Houfe of Commons, into the catalogue of Baronets created by King James, among the Knights of the Bath, nay that he has pried into feveral parliaments, and that no fuch diftinc-tion as a two-fold chriftian name is to be found. What is to be faid to all this? my only reply, fhall be the citation of authorities.

" Richard Maria Dumville, Efq. born anno 1603."
" Huntingdon Haftings Corney, Efq. anno 1603."
                                            " Anna

Anna Maria Eftoufteville, ditto."
" Thomas Maria Wingfield, ap. temp. Edward 6th."

The above names were communicated to me by favor of Francis Townfend, Efq. Windfor Herald.

In a " true report of a late Practife, &c." by Barnabie Riche, 1582, in quarto, black letter, the name of Captain Thomas Maria Wingfield will be found, and is moft probably the perfon, before mentioned. In the Sheldon Pedigree will be obferved Henrietta Maria, daughter of Thomas Savage, Vif. Rock Savage, born 1618. In the will of Sir John White, of Tucksford, in the reign of James the 1ft, the following name appears as a Witnefs. " Welbecke Marke Browneley." In *Lyfon*'s Environs of London, vol. 3, p. 71, it is obferved, that the following baptifmal entry is in the Hornfey Regifter. " Lucius F. Thomæ " Gulielmi ex Louifâ Mariâ, bap. 4. May 1637." Now if Louifa Maria had a fon in May 1637, it is moft probable that fhe was chriftened about the period of the Dramatic Poet. I am alfo furnifhed by Mr. Beltz of the Heralds College, with the chriftian name of Mark Antony, tho' the firname cannot be found. If there is need of further reference, I will cite the name of Henry Frederic,

R   fon

fon of James the Firſt. Nay I will refer to a ſtill
earlier date. In *Lyfon's* Environs, vol. 3, p. 11,
we ſhall find as far back as the year 1416, an in-
ſcripti n in Hendon Church, to the memory of
" John Atte Hevyn."

Surely theſe citations will be ſufficient for my
purpoſe. In faƐt, the uſe of the two-fold chriſtian
names, ſo poſitively and dogmatically objeƐted to
by Mr. Malone, muſt have been a matter of ſuch
undeniable notoriety, that I know not which is the
moſt aſtoniſhing, the unaccountable ſtupidity of
the perſon who overlooked theſe evidences,
or his unparalled effrontery in making ſuch an
aſſertion.

When Mr. Malone obſerves in this exceptionable deed of gift, that the written Plays of
Henry IV. Henry V. King John, King Lear, &c.
are named in the conveyance, he triumphantly exclaims, with his uſual arrogance and inaccuracy,
that the Lear was not written till after OƐtober 24,
1604. The extreme ignorance, diſplayed in this
poſition, is almoſt intolerable. He perſiſts in
ſaying that the Play was written after James was
proclaimed king, *and that was not on the 24th of*
March 1602-3, *but on the 24th of OƐtober* 1604.
So much for accuracy of dates! In reply to this, I
quote Camden's Elizabeth, Book 4, p. 661. which
will clearly prove the ignorance of the critic
on this ſubjeƐt.

" On

" On the 24th of March, 1602-3, being
" the Eve of the Annunciation of the Bleſſed
" Virgin, ſhe (Queen Elizabeth) was called out
" of the priſon of her earthly body, &c. &c.
" The ſad miſs which ſhe left of herſelf to the
" Engliſh, was much leſſened by the great hope
" conceived of the vertues of King James her
" ſucceſſour, who A FEW HOURS AFTER *was pro-*
" *claimed King*, with the joyfull ſhouts and ac-
" clamations of all the people."

" The King" (James of Scotland) " being
" arrived to the 36th year of his reign, continued
" a good correſpondence with Queen Elizabeth,
" as the only way to ſecure his ſucceſſion, ſhe
" having a little before her death, (which hap-
" pened on the 24th of March 1602) declared
" him her ſucceſſor. Whereupon he was THE SAME
" DAY at Whitehall *proclaimed King of England,*
" Scotland, France and Ireland, with great Ac-
" clamations."

Sandford's Hiſtory of England,
Book VII. Chap. I. p. 554.

As to the fatal objection of the indorſement
of the words 2 James, which it ſhould ſeem is
a deciſive proof of the forgery, let me remind the
reader, that it is by no means improbable, that

R 2
the

the deeds were indorfed, a very long period after they were executed, and upon the beft authority I learn that deeds of that period were feldom indor-fed at the time they were drawn. I have fhewn the deed to many antiquaries, and to perfons of the law, verfed in the learning of thefe Papers, who have confirmed this remark. Thefe are all the obfervations, which I fhall make upon the deed, which Mr. Malone has felected as the peculiar victim to his exceptions. What I have faid, will I truft, be found to comprize all that it behoves me to fay upon the fubject. I do not take the defence of the Inftrument upon me any further, than by proving the allegations of Mr. Malone to be fallacious, and unfounded. And it is a rule in logic, that when the negative is difproved, the contrary propofition is eftablifhed.

Now for the *Tributary Lines to Ireland.*

" Oh model of Virtue Charity's fweeteft
" Child, thy Shakfpeare thanks thee
" Nor Verfe, nor Tear can
" paint my Soul nor fay by
" half how much I love thee."

" I beg pardon," exclaims Mr. Malone, (who among other caprices, has affected a ftyle of gallantry) " of all the young ladies of Great Britain
" and

" and Ireland; there is not one of them, fifteen
" years old, who would not produce a better ef-
" fufion after reading the firſt novel, that fell into
" their hands." I folemnly wiſh, that this gentleman, may never have ſtronger reaſons to beg
pardon, and deprecate the anger of the ſex, than
the ſuppoſition, for which he apologizes.

But the next objectionable article, is the view
of Wm. Henry Ireland's houſe, and coat of arms,
&c. It is objectionable on account merely on the
word *View*, being wholly unknown, as he ſays at
the time, in the ſenſe of a delineature of a houſe,
&c. on canvas, paper, or copper. Then as uſual,
he tells us where he has ſearched; and the authorities of lexicographers, and vocabularies, into
which he has examined: though all this does nothing at all, but exhibit an illuſtration of the in-
ſtinct, with which this gentleman is endowed, of
never looking into the proper places.

In Florio's Italian Dictionary printed 1611,
veduta or *viſta* has the Engliſh ſenſe annexed " any
" ſight, view, or proſpect," with other ſynonemes
of the ſame tendency. It is acknowledged by Mr.
Malone, that in this ſenſe the word was uſed in
French ſo early as the ſixteenth century; and it is
not therefore, an aſſumption to ſuppoſe that it ſhould
have crept into our idiom, much earlier, than the
period, to which Mr. Malone attributes it. I ſay
nothing

nothing about the allufion to the fource from which this Haberdafher, as he is contemptuoufly termed, derived his armorial bearings. We all know, that fome of the moft antient families in this country fprung originally from the commercial departments of life ; and perhaps were we to examine the original fountain, whence Mr. Malone derived the arms of his own family we fhould not find them more honorably or unequivocally obtained.

We will now fay a few words on the two coloured drawings, reprefenting the characters of Baffanio, and Shylock: and here, for the firft time, we are furprized with a modeft confeffion on the part of he objector, that he had never feen, what he objects to, and that if he had feen them, he was not entitled by any knowledge of the art to decide upon them. In oppofition to his affertion, that he " has received information from un- " queftionable judges, that they are drawings of " a recent date," I would obferve, that waving my own pretenfions to an accurate knowledge of thefe matters, I appealed to the judgement of Artifts, whom I looked upon as the moft competent to pronounce on the fubject. The uniform opinion of thefe perfons was, that they were the genuine productions of the times, to which they are imputed. In the courfe of feveral months, during which the drawings remained in my pof-

feffion,

feffion, I difcovered an illegible hand-writing, but I was never able to decypher it. On fhewing it however to Mr. Hewlet of the Temple, whom I have mentioned in my preface, that gentleman with the affiftance of glaffes, difcovered the name of Johannes Hofkins, a perfon who at a later period we are told by the late Lord Orford and other writers, became an artift of great merit.

AGREEMENT
Between SHAKSPEARE and LOWINE.

On this head, it appears, that the papers of a Mr. Henflowe, laid before the public in Mr. Malone's laft edition 1793 of Shakfpeare, are appealed to, in oppofition to the validity of the agreement now under confideration. Now, upon the hypothefis of the forgery of the papers, does it not appear very fingular, even to the Critic himfelf, that the fabricator fhould not have reforted to thefe valuable treafures of Mr. Henflowe, efpecially as the greater part of them had been circulated in a book, which might be found in every book-ftall through the country?

However the principal objection is, that John Lowin tho' he fays " his name was fometimes writ-
" ten Lewin, never is to be found *Lowine*." Is it not ftrange, that Mr. Malone, the commentator on Shakfpeare fhould fo heedlefsly convict himfelf of

never

never having looked into the firſt folio Edition of the Great Bard, publiſhed 1623. Let me then inform him, that in the liſt of the actors, he would have found this man's name ſpelt in the objectionable manner. " John Lowine." This is ſurely a bad ſpecimen of Mr. Malone's accuracy. In his claſical way we may ſay, *ab uno crimine diſce* OMNES. When Mr. Malone again quotes a learned language, I would exhort him to be aware of the *diſtinctions of genders*, though it is a ſpecies of learning, in which I am informed, he is not minutely verſed. For *omnes* read *omnia*, as I have before remarked.

The word *Compoſition* is objected to, as to the acceptation that it bears in the agreement, I ſhall refer to no other authorities to juſtify the ſenſe, but that which Mr. Malone himſelf has cited in a note. " Simple is the device, and the *compoſition* " meane." Epiſt. Ded. to Mother Hulbard's Tale, 1590. No one who reads this paſſage, can queſtion the inapplicability of the quotation.

AGREEMENT
BETWEEN SHAKSPEARE AND CONDELL.

The firſt topic that occurs on this head in the ſhape of an objection, is the thread-bare obſervation on the denotation of a guinea " as oune pounde
" and

" and oune fhillynge per week." I fhall not reiter-
ate the reasonings, on which I have entered in a
former part of the work, but I fhall gladly leave
Mr. Malone to the enjoyment of the fulleft triumph that his vanity can derive from fo trivial and
fenfelefs a cavil.

It feems very furprizing to Mr. Malone, that
the falary which Lowine received at the theatre,
fhould have exceeded that of Condell, who ftood
fo high in the eftimation of Shakfpeare and whofe
name ftands as a patentee immediately after that of
Heminges. Whatever might be the rank which
Condell held in the friendfhip of the bard, his
merits as an actor might have been very infignifi-
cant. It is reafonable to prefume that the players
were rewarded according to their profeffional talents at that time, as at prefent. Shakfpeare himfelf we are taught to believe was by no means a
good actor ; and his name might ftill ftand firft as
a principal patentee in the Theatre.

Then we are reminded that from the terms of
the agreement by which he covenants " for three
" years to play upon the ftage, for the faid Wm
" Shakfpeare alle Comedyes ande Tragedves
" which he the faid Wm Shakfpeare may at any
" *tyme during the faid terme caufe to be played not*
" *written or compofed by himfelf butte are the wri-*
" *tings or compofytyons of others* ; from which we muft

S   fuppofe

fuppofe that he would never fuffer one of his own
" pieces to be performed in his own playhoufe, or
" that he bore fuch enmity to Condell, that he had
" made a fixed refolution that he this actor fhould
" not difcharge any part in them." This is the conclufion into which our critic wifhes to precipitate
his readers. But is it an improbable fuppofition
that the covenant was a feparate agreement, for
the exprefs performance of the plays that were not
written by himfelf, and that thofe of his own compofition therefore, had been the fubjects of a diftinct and fpecific agreement. We are then favoured with another conclufion of the ingenious
gentleman, conceived in the true ftyle and genius
of his profound criticifms. This remark only
amounts to this, that he infers the deed of Condell to be fpurious, and that Condell could not
have ufed the peculiar fort of autograph in the MS
becaufe he himfelf in the courfe of his favorite refearches into Parifh Veftries and *Charnel Houfes*,
has not ftumbled upon that actor's autograph.

As to the indorfement of the deed (not to obferve that the indorfement might have been probably made many years after the deed) to the
Englifh form of which Mr. Malone objects, I
fhall refer the reader to feveral authentic deeds
now in the poffeffion of a gentleman, to whom I
have the liberty of referring, fhould any particular
enquiry

enquiry be made on this head. Amongft thefe is an *Englifh Indorfement* in the following deed, viz. A Deed of Gift made in the 22d year of the reign of Henry VI. by John Cannyeforde to John Wolfele of landed property at Trowbridge Wilts. The Deed is in Latin, and Cannyeforde is there defcribed *Clericus* ; and the indorfement is as follows. " John " Kannyeforde *Clark*." There is alfo another deed of gift dated 28th Edward III. in Latin from Wm. Heye to Philippo le Schephurde, and it is indorfed in Englifh thus " 28th Edward third, Phl. le " Schephurd." Among innumerable other deeds with the citation of which I fhall not overwhelm the faculties of the reader, I have felected thefe, which I truft will fhew very fully that there are exifting indorfements in Englifh to deeds of the period, on which we are now occupied.

The Leafe to Michael Frafer next comes under animadverfion. Upon this head I fhall not detain the reader very long. But I might advert with juftifiable feverity to the farcaftic allufion made by the critic to the perfons who fubfcribed to the work. Their rank in life and the literary reputation of the greater part, whofe names adorn the catalogue, are far above the reach of any ridicule that Mr. Malone can direct againft them. But the critic's principal objection is this ; *that the Globe on the Southwark fide of the Thames,* is de-

S 2   fcribed

fcribed to be by *Black Friars, London.* Upon
this fubject I fhall fay but little; not feeling it my
duty to difcourfe at large upon all the wire-fpun.
and trivial cavils that a critic like Mr. Malone is
able to bring forward. I produced the deed in
the prefence of many intelligent perfons, who
were of opinion that the word (*by*) fhould be
conftrued with a greater latitude of meaning, than
Mr. Malone feems to allow it; and that it fignifies general vicinity, rather than a ftrict proximity.
And here I will make one general obfervation,
which the candid reader will apply to other parts
of the MS. I would remark that amongft a mul-
tifarious mafs of papers, like thofe in my poffeffion, it would be abfurd to fuppofe that fome
would not furnifh matter of petty quibble, and
exception to thofe minds, which are not fuffi-
ciently comprehenfive to embrace general arguments, or purfue general reafonings upon thefe
fubjects.

And now we are approaching that, which Mr.
Malone ftyles to be worfe than the " thickeft
" Cimmerian darknefs," the deed of truft to John
Hemynges. They who are converfant with the
critic's powers of illuftrating and penetrating ob-
fcurities, will be rather furprized that he fhould
have any objection to that, with which he is fo
very familiar. Every animal is endued with natural

tural organs adapted to the element in which it lives ; and I have always thought, that black letter criticks and commentators who feem to breathe only in darknefs, never enjoyed repofe 'till they had brought their author's fenfe and meaning to the mift and obfcurity of their own underftandings and apprehenfions.

But let us endeavour to ftate concifely one or two of Mr. Malone's objections. The firft is, that the deed fets out with informing us, that at the time at which the deed is dated, Shakfpeare had not yet returned into the country. The deed of mortgage in the next year (March 10th and 11th, 1612-13) is adduced by Mr. Malone to invalidate the pofition. On this head I have only to remark that the objection is not fupported by the mortgage deed; becaufe the intervening year would have afforded Shakfpeare ample time for the retirement to which the critic refers.

Then it is animadverted on, as improbable, that the deed fhould have opened in thefe words, " having found muche wickednefs amongft thofe " of the lawe, &c." very unlikely fays Mr. Malone, that he fhould have had fo low an opinion of lawyers, when he was in habits of friendfhip with feveral members of that profeffion. What incongruity and what inconfiftency is there in this ? Why does Mr. Malone infer, that becaufe our

bard

bard had a few connexions in that profeffion, for whom he had the higheft efteem and refpect, he could not have entertained a general impreffion againft the character of the body in general ? The objector ought to have known alfo, that there are a variety of paffages in the works of Shakfpeare, in which he has put into the mouths of his perfonages many very fevere and ftriking animadverfions on the body, againft which Mr. Malone thinks it impoffible, that he could have imbibed any diflike or prepoffeffion.

Thefe are fpecimens of his reafonings upon the deed of truft to Heminges, with which I fuppofe the reader will be perfectly fatisfied. He has indeed favoured us with many other obfervations, drawn from the armoury of antiquarian and legal refearches, with which I fhall not condefcend to interfere. My purpofe was not that of purfuing Mr. Malone through all the dark avenues and fubterraneous apartments of the gothick edifice of reafoning, which he has erected with fuch infinite labour and diligence.

Mr. Malone, p. 300, with refpect to the child mentioned in the deed, to whofe ufe the eight plays are appropriated, fays that he " prefumes the " child to be Shakfpeare's god-fon young William " D'Avenant; and " I fear," fays he, " that I am " anfwerable for his having been brought for-
" ward."

" ward." So that the critic acknowledges himself guilty of what has not been laid to his charge, viz. of having brought a bantling into the world. I sincerely hope that Mr. Malone will have the grace to erase the confession of the illicit and wanton ways of which he pleads guilty, in his future editions of Shakspeare.

But because I have not entered into all the abstruse arguments, in which he has bewildered himself and his readers, it would be an unfair inference to draw, that I have not succeeded in the object of this work, which was that of exposing the greater part of the fallacies, errors, sophisms, and impertinent cavils with which he has attempted to impose on the world, in the shape of critical investigations. Let the topics I have selected, serve as a general specimen of the style of his writing and the force of his arguments. Let the public judge by the articles I have examined, of the rest of those broken wares and mouldy commodities, he has exposed to sale.

I have now finished my observations on that part of Mr. Malone's work, which respects the deeds and documents. I shall now only trespass on the patience of the reader, with a few remarks on the *Lear* and the *Hamlet*.

Here the Critic sets out with an ingenuous avowal of his being utterly disqualified for the dif-

cuffion

cuſſion of the ſubjeȼt. He obſerves that he has
not collated a ſingle line of the Lear, except one
ſpeech; and that life would be too ſhort for the
examination of ſuch traſh, when a ſingle glance is
ſufficent to ſhew it to be a plain and palpable forgery. Yet it might be imagined, that he whoſe
whole life has been ſpent in the taſk, to the drudgery of which he now takes ſuch an extraordinary
averſion, would not have felt much repugnance to
the minute and ſlender inquiries of collating, and
exploring the paſſages on which he notwithſtanding
preſumes to give a deciſive, and oracular opinion.
" Three words" ſays he, " will ſuffice on the ſub-
" jeȼt." Yet theſe three words, multiplying
themſelves like the polypi, are made to fill nearly
twenty pages of his volume.

As to the ſingle paſſage he has ſeleȼted, I
ſhall ſay a few words.

Alb. " Whats the matterre Sir."
Leare. " Marke mee Ile tell the life and death I amme
" aſhamed thou haſt powerre to ſhake mye manhood
" thuſſe, that theſe hotte teares that breake fromme mee
" perforce ſhould make worſe blaſts and foggs
" onne the unnetennedere woundinges of a fatherres *curſe*
" *Eyſſe* playe thys part agayne Ile plucke ye oute and caſte
" you with the waterres that you maye temperre claye.''

Allowing Mr. Malone the incorreȼtneſs of the
ſpeech as it ſtood, I by no means admit it to be
a fair

a fair ftandard by which the reft is to be eftimated.

In the fixth line, after the word *fathers*, *curfe* is
unqueftionably omitted, and in the next line *uſſe* is
an error inftead of *Eyſſe*, as it ftands in the MS.
Thefe are errors of tranfcription for which I am
alone accountable, but if the reader with thefe cor-
rections will perufe the paſſage, I am perfuaded that
it will appear in a light totally different, if not a real
emendation of the vulgar text.

But let me befeech the reader to attend to the
following lines in the MS (the fpeech of Kent in
the laft fcene), which Mr. Malone obferves that
any fchool boy might have written.

> *Kente.* " Thanks Sir butte I goe toe thatte unknowne
> lande.
> " Thatte chaynes each Pilgrim fafte within its foyle
> " Bye livynge menne mofte fhunn'd moufte dreadedde
> " Stille mye goode mafterre this fame journey tooke
> " He calls me I amme contente and ftrayght obeye
> " Thenne farewelle worlde the bufye fceane is done
> " Kente liv'd moufte true Kente dyes moufte lyke a
> " manne."

I make no comment upon thefe lines, though
I cannot abftain from remarking, that he who
compares this emendation with the following fpeech
of Kent, as it exifts in the other editions,

T   " I haue

" I haue a journey, Sir, fhortly to go ;
" My mafter calls me, I muft not fay, no."

and does not pronounce it to be replete with pathos
and energy, muft refign all pretenfions to critical
difcernment as well as poetical tafte. The above
paffage has received the commendations of all who
have read it; and it is much more eafy, after
the fpecimen he has given us of his tafte and eru-
dition, to fuppofe that Mr. Malone is not endued
with the flighteft particle of either, than that the
beft fcholars of the age fhould have given their
fuffrage in favor of lines, which any fchool boy
might have written.

We are next told, as an objection to the papers, that the method of numbering the lines, is
unauthorized by the ufage of Shakfpeare and the
time in which he wrote. Here we have once
more an unauthorized affertion. Is Mr. Malone to
impofe the tenet of the Pythagorean School on his
difciples ? Is every pofition, which falls from his
pen, to be received with implicit reverence, on
matters of controverfy like the prefent? Has
this gentleman in his poffeffion any of the original
MSS of Shakfpeare, to fhew the fpecific ufage of
the bard in this refpect? If he has not, upon
what ground does his inference reft ? The fame
obfervation will apply to the circumftance of the

plays,

plays, having been written on one fide only of the paper. It may be further remarked, that at that time, thefe ufages muft have been variable, and uncertain, and I would obferve that as far as the latter objection goes it is invalid, becaufe many of the MSS. in my poffeffion contain the writing on both fides, which Mr. Malone pofitively afferts, the quality of the paper would not admit of.

At the clofe of thefe remarks, we are prefented with an argument, which it would furely perplex our modern logicians, and thofe who are verfed in the prevailing forms of reafoning, to analyze, and examine. " The outworks being demolifhed the " fort muft furrender," in plain Englifh, having laid down in a mafs of accumulated affertion, that the other writings, whether love letters, addreffes to his patron, or copies of verfes, are a collection of unintelligible nonfenfe, the Play of Vortigern, which he had not read, nor feen, nor examined, muft be unintelligible nonfenfe likewife. This is the new fafhioned fyllogifm, with which the garrulous commentator has finifhed his obfervations on the fubject of the amended plays, lately prefented to the world. I have adverted to it, that the reader may fee the uniform tenor of the learned gentleman's reafoning, and obferve the admirable correfpondence and unity of ftructure and defign, that prevails through the whole

T 3   of

of his inquiry from the firft to the laft page of his book.

As to the whole length portrait of Shakfpeare in oil, and the uncut two firft folios, farcaftically alluded to by Mr. Malone, I have nothing to remark farther, than that the communication was made to me by my fon, and that all the information I ever received concerning them, refts on his authority. As a proof of Mr. Malone's accuracy with refpect to the facts advanced in his book, he talks (in a note), of a letter in which Shakfpeare fpeaks highly of *Vortigern* and infifts on a larger price for the copyright of it than his bookfeller was willing to give him. On this I have to remark, that the letter alluded to, does not fpecify *Vortigern*, nor does it bear any appearance of its alluding to that play at all. This will ferve for as good a fpecimen of the critic's faculty of dreaming, as that with which he has favoured us at the conclufion of his volume.

To fhew the facility, with which an impofture of this kind might be conducted, the critic cites an inftance of his own patience and labor, in the execution of a tafk which he prefcribed to himfelf, of copying out the whole poem of Romeus and Juliet, in three days. This however proves only what the laborious texture of Mr. Malone's mind is capable of fuftaining. It is a capacity which I do not mean to deny him in common, with

with every stationer's apprentice and clerk in the kingdom. With the same pains and diligence he might have copied the Iliad, without being able to interpret a single character of the Greek language, or Euclid's works, without knowing a single proposition in mathematics. But does this instance of persevering dulness apply to the mass of papers before us; in which not only manual industry, but manual dexterity, and identity of fiction, and no ordinary powers of mind are uniformly displayed, upon the hypothesis of its being an imposture?

But this collection of remarks, egotisms, and conjectures at length seems to approach its termination. Mr. Malone has displayed all the varieties of the human faculty in the course of his enquiry: he has been the critic, the wit, the antiquary, the scholar, the man of gallantry. But what ought to exhibit the singular dexterity of Mr. Malone in acting the several parts he has assumed, is the circumstance that nature has denied him all the qualities requisite for the task; just as it would be a surprising feat of dexterity, if a man were to dance the rope without legs; for he is at once a critic without taste, a poet without imagination, a scholar without learning, a wit without humour, an antiquary without the least knowledge of antiquity, and *a man of gallantry, without*————

But

But the art in which he poffeffes a truly admirable faculty, is that of *Dreaming.* Over dreams he poffeffes an unlimited dominion; and he feems like the God of Dreams in Virgil, furrounded with all the drowfy powers and agents, which thronged in the eternal abode of filence and fleep.

After having tried the powers of his art in lulling his readers to fleep, through the courfe of feveral hundred pages, he concludes with a long account of his own dream, which for the amufement of my readers, I fhall attempt to analyze and examine.

In a collection of marvellous ftories, known by the name of Wanley's Wonders of the littleWorld, as well as in Quevedo's celebrated vifions, we have many very remarkable ftories of dreams. But the dream of Mr. Malone is fo extraordinary, that it out-wonders all the wonders, that ever were recorded in any book whatever. Dreams are faid to be copies of our waking impreffions. This dream is therefore the more wonderful, as it cannot poffibly be prefumed to be a copy of any waking impreffion, that ever vifited the underftanding of Mr. Malone, for he dreams, Gentle Reader, that he is tranfported to Parnaffus, and fitting as counfel for Shakfpeare, among Apollo and his nine Sifters ! ! ! and it is not to be fuppofed that this gentleman had ever any waking notions of

making

making an excurfion to Parnaffus, and he is too modeft and deficient to obtrude himfelf into the fociety of nine ladies, with whom he has fo flight an acquaintance.

Then after a beautiful and fanciful defcription of the immortal bards in Elyfium, who it feems were employed in practifing upon their fiddles, the dreamer at laft finds out the great dramatic poet playing at bowls with Spencer, Suckling and Hales. What is more remarkable ftill, he finds him out by his refemblance to a picture in the poffeffion of the Duke of Chandos, " *three copies* " *of which are in my poffeffion.*" Here however, the dreamer has forgot what one of his fraternity has fo fully proved with fo much ingenuity and learning, namely, that it bears no refemblance at all to the authentic engraving of Droefhout, which has received the teftimony of Ben Jonfon. But that our immortal bard, who was the plaintiff in the fuit, on the trial of which Mr. Malone was engaged as counfel, fhould be playing a game at bowls, is another aftonifhing proof of the extraordinary gift of dreaming, with which the critic is endued. Virgil defcribes the departed fpirits in Elyfium as occupied in the concerns and amufements with which they were gratified when alive. But the peep of our critic into thofe regions, will for the future correct the error of the antient mythology,

thology, from which Virgil derived his notion, unlefs Mr. Malone intends to gratify the world with a tract to prove from fome of the documents *in his poffeffion,* that Shakfpeare, Suckling and Spencer were very fond of playing at the game of bowls or nine-pins.

But perhaps it is quite as remarkable that Shakfpeare fhould have required the affiftance of a counfel to appear in his behalf before Apollo and the Mufes ; and that he fhould have fent for Mr. Malone from the other world to undertake his defence. If it was neceffary the caufe fhould have been entrufted to a commentator, Apollo might have found out a crowd of critics, black letter compilers, and lexicographers, nay his old friends, Cotgrave, Minchen, Barret and Phillips. But one might have thought that amongft the facred groupes, that thronged in thofe celeftial regions, there would be no dearth of advocates in the caufe of fo diftinguifhed a bard. Milton, Spenfer, Cowley and Pope, would furely have been called into court inftead of Mr. Malone, to protect the violated rights and the facred reputation of a member of their own corporation, who one would have thought has fuffered too much from the difputes of critics and commentators, to rely much upon their efforts in his caufe.

Here I clofe my obfervations on the dream of
Mr.

Mr. Malone; and in the courfe of this pamphlet, I hope I fhall have proved, that as a critic and a fcholar, Mr. Malone is entitled to an equal degree of attention, whether he dreams or whether he is awake.

And here I would exhort the reader not to confider me as an advocate for the authenticity of the controverted MSS. The tafk of refuting the reafonings of Mr. Malone is diftinct from that of eftablifhing either the affirmative or negative propofition on this doubtful and myfterious queftion. I wifh to defend the caufe of literature and of found criticifm, which are effectually wounded if dogmatic affertions, infinuations, and mifreprefentations are allowed to triumph over folid and fubftantial inveftigation. It would be a labour infinitely above my ability, though the very attempt would ennoble the meaneft capacity, *melioribus humeris fuftinendum*, to deftroy the fpirit of vague and conjectural criticifm, which has ravaged the fields of poetry, imagination and fcience. How far I have fucceeded, is a point on which I fhall not prefume to determine; and I clofe the fubject with the fatisfactory confcioufnefs, that in appealing to the world, I have laid the merits of my caufe, before that tribunal, which will not fuffer the voice of truth to be overwhelmed and extinguifhed.

F I N I S.

ADDENDA.

THE word *Master*, which Mr. Malone says was never thus spelt in the time of Elizabeth, will be found in the title to " *Fortescue's new Book in Commendation of the Laws of England, printed in* 1599, " Written in Latin by the learned and right honorable *Master* Fortescue, Knt."

Grafton's Chronicle, printed in 1569, has in the Epistle Dedicatory to Sir William Cecil, Knt. the Word, *Mastership* and *Maistership*, thus differently spelt in the same page.

For instances of double Christian names, I am favored with the following, since this work was printed.

Henry Roger Boyle, died in 1615 : See Lyson's London, Vol. 4, p. 365.

Eyton John Seymour ; See Visitation of Berkshire.

William Robards Smith, anno 1604, Blomfield's Norfolk, Vol. 3, p. 584.

ERRATA.

Page 31, *line* 8, *for* 1354, *read* 1534.
32, — 18, *for* Cotrave, *read* Cotgrave. Bullekar, *read* Bullokar and *in* Sherrwood, *dele the second* r.
35, *last line but two, for* in, *read* or to.
36, — 10, *for* Cronicle, *read* Chronicle.
43, — 21, *after* his work, *read* he says.
51, — 16, *for* similiar, *read* similar.
81, — 3, *for* rationai, *read* rational.
136, — 19, *for* Hubard *read* Hubbard.

APPENDIX

A

REPLY

TO AN

ENQUIRY, &c.

––––––––––

THE greateſt difficulty which I have to en-
counter, in my examination of Mr. Malone's
work, is that which ariſes from the ſuperfluous
matter, with which it abounds. The advantage
which that author derives, from this redundant and
deſultory method of purſuing his ſubject, is very
obvious. If he does not overpower his adver-
ſaries, he at leaſt overwhelms his readers. They,
who take up the book, not indeed from its bulk,
but from the amplitude of its materials, are diſ-
poſed to feel a prepoſſeſſion in its favour; for
where much labor has been obviouſly beſtowed,
ſome learning is neceſſarily inferred. Thus the
greater part of its readers yield a ſtupid aſſent, and
are too much perplexed into acquieſcence; becauſe
they are willing to give the author credit for having
proved that, which their own indolence will not
ſuffer them to examine.

A   Before

Before however, the opinions of any critic are examined, it is proper to fee, whether he has any right to maintain an opinion at all. On what grounds does the critical competence of Mr. Malone reft? In the beginning of his work he declares that he refufed to infpect the papers; that he rejected every invitation for that purpofe. He has himfelf pleaded his own difqualification.

All human opinion is the refult of antecedent enquiry; and any opinion on any fpecific queftion, may be pronounced folid, or ill founded, according to the means and opportunities, which he who maintains it has had of enquiring into the evidence relative to it. Different queftions require different evidence, and are tried by different fenfes; but on queftions concerning certain vifible and material inftruments, infpection is the only ftandard to which reference is to be made. The eye alone examines into the evidence, becaufe it is only by the eye, that minute analogies can be remarked, and comparifons of colors, fhades, and refemblances fairly and accurately made. Mr. Malone fays that he difdained to try this queftion by perfonal infpection. He rejected the only fair, and fatisfactory method of arriving at a judgment upon the papers. Mr. Malone has therefore proved himfelf very incompetent to pronounce concerning their merits.

It

EIGHTEENTH CENTURY SHAKESPEARE

During the one hundred and seven years covered by this series, the reputation of William Shakespeare as poet and dramatist rose from a controversial and highly qualified acceptance by post-Restoration critics and "improvers" to the almost idolatrous admiration of the early Romantics and their immediate precursors. Imposing its own standards and interpretations upon Shakespeare, the Eighteenth Century scrutinized his work in various lights. Certain qualities of the plays were isolated and discussed by a parade of learned, cantankerous, and above all self-assured commentators.

Thirty-five of the most important and representative books and pamphlets are here presented in twenty-six volumes; many of the works, through the very fact of their limited circulation have become extremely scarce, and when obtainable, expensive and fragile. The series will be useful not only for the student of Shakespeare's reputation in the period, but for all those interested in eighteenth century taste, taste-making, scholarship, and theatre. Within the series we may follow the arguments and counter-arguments as they appeared to contemporary playgoers and readers, and the shifting critical emphases characteristic of the whole era.

In an effort to provide responsible texts of these works, strict editorial principles have been established and followed. All relevant editions have been compared, the best selected, and the reasons for the choice given. Furthermore, at least one other copy, frequently three or more, have been collated with the copy actually reproduced, and the collations recorded. In cases where variants or cancels exist, every attempt has been made to provide both earlier and later or indifferently varying texts, as appendices. Each volume is preceded by a short preface discussing the text, the publication history, and, when necessary, critical and biographical considerations not readily available.

Play-wrighte, Maister Williaume Shakespere, from the Maney
Errours, faulsely charged on him, by Certaine New-fangled
Wittes and to let him speak for Himself, as right well he
wotteth, when Freede from the many Careless Mistakeings, of
the Heedless first Imprinters, of his Workes (1749)
94p.   55s.

7. 1748 **Thomas Edwards**
The Canons of Criticism and Glossary. Being a Supplement
to Mr. Warburton's Edition of Shakespear. Collected from
the Notes in that celebrated Work, and proper to be bound
up with it. To which are added, The Trial of the Letter *Y*
alias Y; and Sonnets (Seventh Edition, with Additions 1765)
368p.   £5 5s.

8. 1748 **Peter Whalley**
An Enquiry into the Learning of Shakespeare (1748)
84p.
   1767 **Richard Farmer**
As Essay on the Learning of Shakespeare . . . the Second
Edition, with Large Additions (1767)
viii, 96p.   70s.

9. 1752 **William Dodd**
The Beauties of Shakespeare: Regularly selected from each
Play, With a General Index, Digesting them under Proper
Heads. Illustrated with Explanatory Notes and Similar
Passages from Ancient and Modern Authors (1752)
2v., xxiv, 264; iv, 258p.   £10 10s.

10. 1753 **Charlotte Ramsay Lennox**
Shakespear Illustrated . . . with Critical Remarks (1753-4)
3v., xiv, 292; iv, 276; iv, 312p.   £15

11. 1765 **William Kenrick**
A Review of Doctor Johnson's New Edition of Shakespeare:
In which the Ignorance, or Inattention of That Editor is
exposed, and the Poet Defended from the Persecution of his
Commentators (1765)
xvi, 136p.
    1766 **Thomas Tyrwhitt**
Observations and Conjectures upon some Passages of

Shakespeare (1766)
ii, 56p.   75s.

12. 1769 **Elizabeth Montagu**
An Essay on the Writings and Genius of Shakespear, compared with the Greek and French dramatic Poets. With some
remarks upon the misrepresentations of Mons. de Voltaire
(1769)
iv, 288p.   90s.

13. 1774 **William Richardson**
    1784 Essays on Shakespeare's Dramatic Characters: With an
    1789 Illustration of Shakespeare's Representation of National
Character, in that of Fluellen (sixth edition 1812)
xii, 448p.   £6 6s.

14. 1775 **Elizabeth Griffith**
The Morality of Shakespeare's Drama Illustrated (1775)
xvi, 528p.   £9 9s.

15. 1777 **Maurice Morgann**
An Essay on the Dramatic Character of Sir John Falstaff
(1777)
xii, 186p.   63s.

16. 1783 **Joseph Ritson**
Remarks Critical and Illustrative of the last Edition of
Shakespeare [by George Steevens, 1778], (1783)
viii, 240p.
    1788 **Joseph Ritson**
The Quip Modest; A few Words by way of Supplement to
Remarks, Critical and Illustrative on the Text and Notes of
the Last Edition of Shakespeare: occasioned by a Republi-
cation of that Edition (1788, first issue)
viii, 32p.
With the preface (revised) to the second issue of *The Quip
Modest* (1788)
viii p.   84s.

17. 1785 **Thomas Whately**
Remarks on some of the Characters of Shakespere, Edited

by Richard Whately (Third edition 1839)
128p.   55s.

18. 1785 **John Monck Mason**
     1797 Comments on the Several Editions of Shakespeare's Plays,
     1798 Extended to those of Malone and Steevens (1807)
           xvi, 608p.   £9 9s.

19. 1786 **John Philip Kemble**
           Macbeth and King Richard the Third: An Essay, in answer to
           Remarks on some of the Characters of Shakespeare [by
           Thomas Whately] (1817)
           xii, 172p.   63s.

20. 1792 **Joseph Ritson**
           Cursory Criticisms on the Edition of Shakespeare published
           by Edmond Malone (1792)
           x, 104p.
           Edmond Malone
           A Letter to the Rev. Richard Farmer, D.D. Master of
           Emanuel College, Cambridge; Relative to the Edition of
           Shakespeare, published in 1790. And Some Late Criticisms
           on that work (1792)
           ii, 40p.   60s.

21. 1796 **William Henry Ireland**
           An Authentic Account of the Shakespeare Manuscripts (1796)
           ii, 44p.
     1799 **William Henry Ireland**
           Vortigern, An Historical Tragedy, In five Acts; Represented
           at the Theatre Royal, Drury Lane. And Henry the Second,
           An Historical Drama. Supposed to be written by the Author
           of Vortigern (1799)
           80, iv, 79p.   75s.

22. 1796 **Edmond Malone**
           An Inquiry into the Authenticity of Certain Miscellaneous
           Papers and Legal Instruments, published Dec. 24, 1795. And
           Attributed to Shakespeare, Queen Elizabeth, and Henry
           Earl of Southampton (1796)
           vii, 424p.   £7

23. 1796 **Thomas Caldecott**
Mr. Ireland's Vindication of his Conduct, Respecting the Publication of the Supposed Shakespeare Manuscripts (1796)
iv, 48p.

1800 **George Hardinge**
Chalmeriana: or a Collection of Papers ... occasioned by reading a late Apology for the Believers in the Shakespeare papers, by George Chalmers etc. (1800)
viii, 94p.   60s.

24. 1798 **Samuel Ireland**
An Investigation of Mr. Malone's Claim to the Character of Scholar, or Critic, Being an Examination of his Inquiry into the Authenticity of the Shakespeare Manuscripts, etc. (1797)
vi, 156p.   63s.

25. 1797 **George Chalmers**
An Apology for the Believers in the Shakespeare-Papers which were exhibited in Norfolk Street (1797)
iv, 628p.   £9 9s.

26. 1799 **George Chalmers**
A Supplemental Apology for the Believers in the Shakespeare-Papers: Being a Reply to Mr. Malone's Answer, which was early announced, but never published: with a Dedication to George Steevens, and a Postscript (1799)
viii, 656 p.   £9 9s.

For Product Safety Concerns and Information please contact our EU
representative GPSR@taylorandfrancis.com
Taylor & Francis Verlag GmbH, Kaufingerstraße 24, 80331 München, Germany